History of Urbanization

A Study on Landscape and Contemporary History of

Nainital

History of Urbanization

A Study on Landscape and Contemporary History of

Nainital

Reetesh Sah

ANAMIKA PUBLISHERS & DISTRIBUTORS (P) LTD.
4697/3, 21A, Ansari Road, Daryaganj, New Delhi 110 002
Phones: 011-2328 1655, 011-43708938
E-mail: anamikapublishers@yahoo.co.in

First Published 2022

ISBN 978-81-7975-799-4

PRINTED IN INDIA

Published by Anamika Publishers & Distributors (P) Ltd., 4697/3, 21A, Ansari Road, Daryaganj, New Delhi 110 002. Typeset by Aadil Printographics, Delhi 110092 and Printed at Vikas Computer & Printers, Tronica City, Ghaziabad

Contents

Foreword

The British occupied Kumaon and Garhwal in 1815 and developed Naini Tal as a health and recreational resort after 1841. G.W. Traill, the second Commissioner of British Kumaon who had a good knowledge of Indian culture was the first British to have visited the place in 1823 but he did not want Europeans to know about it owing to its divine sanctity. P. Barron who is credited to have come here first in 1841was helpful in popularizing Naini Tal and facilitated the process of urbanization. In 1856, the Commissioner's office was transferred from Almora to Nainital owing to its salubrious climate and proximity to the plains, which gave boost to its popularity. It assumed a new importance in 1857, as a safe place for the British refugees as there was no outbreak of disorder here during that period. In 1862, Naini Tal became the summer seat of the North Western Provinces. After it was made the summer capital, a remarkable expansion of the town occurred with the setting up of the Secretariat and other administrative units.

On 15th October 1891 Naini Tal became a district owing to its administrative importance. In 1908 the summer seat of the Chemical Laboratory was established here. It also became famous as an important centre of education for the British who wanted to educate their children in better air and away from the discomfort of the plains, not to mention the risks of living in the south after the uprising of 1857. By the turn of the century Naini Tal became a famous tourist centre and after Independence as a centre of administration. With the formation of the Uttarakhand State, the town was embellished with the establishment of the High Court of Uttarakhand in Naini Tal and the Uttarakhand Academy of Administration for the training of bureaucrats.

Dr. Reetesh Sah has made an innovative endeavour by tracing the history, growth and urban development of this hill town. His work is based totally on primary sources supplemented by books and other secondary material. He has the art to disarm and capture his readers and widen their horizon with a new perspective. His work on Nainital has become alive with seeds of primary sources and I hope it shall make waves among historians, gripping the intelligent readers to forget food and sleep. He has made the work more interesting by writing on the shrines of Nainital and the communal harmony they portray. The beauty of Nainital is that the Temple, Gurudwara, Mosque, Arya Samaj Mandir and Church etc. are in close proximity to each other.

He has also made an interesting probe into the ecological sensitivity of the town interwoven with the history of landslides which struck Nainital during the 19th century. Subsequent upon the landslip of1867, the British Government constituted the Hillside Safety Committee and after the diabolic landslide of 1880 constructed 79 km. length of nullahs; a unique drainage system in the catchment area of Naini Lake, which has saved the town from destruction hitherto.

Dr. Reetesh has also unfolded the detrimental impact of urbanization and the remedial measures undertaken by the administration like aeration, bio-manipulation, removing encroachment upon the nullahs, dumping of garbage at the entry point of Nainital etc. after the decision of the Hon'ble Supreme Court and of the Hon'ble High Court of Uttarakhand.

Prof. Ajay Singh Rawat

Preface

Historical sign of urban planning are referred to the most urbanized Harappan civilization in the 3rd millennium BCE. Archeological studies of the ruins in the cities in these areas find paved streets that were laid out at right angles in a set pattern. The idea of a planned out urban area evolved as different civilizations adopted it. Ancient Greek and Roman also adopted idea of Urban Planning. This impact is clearly visible in the towns developed by the Europeans in their colonies. Under the colonial rule, European rulers especially British, developed many towns. After controlling administration of India the British not only developed several towns for administrative purposes but also urbanized new towns for themselves.

Nainital is one among the towns which was urbanized by the Colonial Rulers. Discovered in 1841 AD and soon after establishment of a Municipal Board, several rules and regulation were laid down to develop this town in a managed way. The process of urbanization in Nainital town at that time of development was a complex phenomenon that is affected by the physical, cultural, social, religious and economic structure of the region. In

Lesser Himalayas most of the habitat centers were developed, particularly in the Kumaun region, owing to its unique physico-cultural and economic conditions, the process of urbanization has been slower than most of other regions of the country. Not only their number but also the size of these towns is small. Even then, they play an important role in changing and patterning the socio-economic aspects of the region.

In the initial years of its habitation, Nainital was developed as a beautiful and well managed town. The British government created infrastructure and services in the town. Nainital was developed by the British with a specific vision of perfect planning. During their rule the Colonial rulers consider Nainital as a part of England.

But faulty planning and lopsided approach towards urban planning in Post-Independence period shattered the initial vision of urbanization of this town. The impact of human intervention on the infrastructure and problems created by the illegal construction as well as unrestrained vehicular traffic, lack of public facilities, parks, parking areas, public welfare, cleanliness and pollution increased problems in the township. The builders cashing in on the great demand for new houses have scarred the tender and lovely hill side and constructed houses, guest houses and huge hotels in localities which were declared unsafe and where such activities were strictly prohibited by the British and Municipal Bye-Laws. Rubble from the construction site was not removed but dumped into the lake during the rains through drain channels, which accelerated the rate of sedimentation.

The major findings of this study point to the comprehensive urban development vulnerability assessment. And mapping of the town should be carried out, taking into account all the critical parameters of exposure, sensitivity, and adaptive capacity of the urban planning. A dynamic and comprehensive blue print for Nainital is needed which is specifically responsive to its unique geographical and ecological setting. Emphasis needs to be placed on strengthening of historic urban planning.

Reetesh Sah

Acknowledgement

The extensive study conducted for the purpose of this book included interaction with officials, citizens and representatives from various walks of life through interviews and other modes of communication in Nainital. The author would like to sincerely thank them for their time and inputs. I would like to thank local historians and academicians for their support in putting vital inputs for this book. Several senior citizens provided responses for the book which helped in enhancing its qualitative aspects. I thank My Mother Mrs. Champa Sah, Wife Mrs. Mallika Sah, Son Aviral Sah, Brother Mr. Ratnesh Sah his wife Vibha and their daughters Katyayni & Varnika and all family members for their affectionate support. I am thankful to Prof. Ajay Singh Rawat for his perennial inspiration, motivation and blessings to take on this task; I am thankful to all my colleagues and friends for their motivation and cooperation and last but not the least Anamika Publishers, New Delhi for publishing this book.

Reetesh Sah

List of Abbreviations

AD	Anno Domini
BC	Before Christ
BCE	Before Common Era
BOD	Biological Oxygen Demand
CDP	City Development Plan
Col.	Colonel
Lt.	Lieutenant
MB	Municipal Board
NLRSADA	Nainital Lake Region Special Area Development Authority
NWP	North West Province
PWD	Public Works Department
SDM	Sub Divisional Magistrate
SWM	Solid Waste Management
m.	Meters
Km^2	Square kilometer
NIH	National Institute of Hydrology
MBT	Main Boundary Thrust
LCFPS	Lee Commission Free Passage Scheme
ULB	Urban Local Body

CHAPTER-1

Introduction

Historical evidence of urban planning dates back to the Harappan civilization in the third millennium BCE. Archeological studies of the ruins in these cities, found paved streets that were laid out at right angles in a grid pattern. The idea of a planned out urban area was evolved and later different civilizations adopted it accordingly. Beginning in the 8th century BCE, Greek cities were primarily centered on orthogonal or grid-like plans. The ancient Romans, inspired by the Greeks, also used orthogonal plans for their cities. City planning in the Roman world was developed for military purposes and public convenience. The spread of the Roman Empire subsequently spread the ideas of urban planning as well. As the Roman Empire declined, this idea faded slowly. However, many cities in Europe later followed the system like planned the Roman city center. Cities in Europe from the 9th to 14^{th}centuries often grew organically and sometimes chaotically. Many of towns were newly built according to preconceived plans, and many others were enlarged with newly planned extensions and most of these came into existence from the 12th to 14th centuries.

From the 15th century onwards, much is recorded about the urban design and the people were involved in designing the towns. In this period, theoretical treatises on architecture and urban planning start to appear in which theoretical questions are addressed and designs of towns and cities are described and depicted. During the Enlightenment period, several European rulers ambitiously attempted to redesign capital cities.

The laissez-faire style of government management of the economy, in fashion for most of the Victorian era, was started to give way to a New Liberalism that championed intervention on the part of the poor and disadvantaged. Theorists began developing urban planning models to mitigate the consequences of the industrial age, by providing citizens, especially the factory workers, with healthier environments. But here in India the urbanization process was focused on the need of the British administration and to help them to live in better environment which could offer feel of their mother land that was miles away from this part of the world, which they urbane recently.

This impact is clearly visible in the towns developed by the Europeans in their colonies. Under the colonial rule European rulers especially the British developed many towns. After controlling the administration of India the British not only developed several towns for the administrative purpose but also discovered new towns for their leisure settlement.

Urban planning is a technical and political process concerned with the development and use of land, planning permission, protection and the use of environment, public welfare, and the design of urban environment, including air, water,and the infrastructure passing into and out of urban areas, such as transportation, communications, and distribution of networks. Urban planning is also referred to as urban and regional planning, town planning, city planning, rural planning or some combination in various areas worldwide. It takes many forms and it can share perspectives and practices with urban design.

Urban planning guides orderly development in urban and suburban areas. Although predominantly concerned with the planning of settlements and communities, urban planning is also responsible for the planning and development of water use and other resources, rural and agricultural land, parks and conserving areas of natural environmental significance. Practitioners of urban planning are concerned with research and analysis, strategic thinking, architecture, urban design, public consultation, policy recommendations, implementation and management. The British adopted urban planning in the study area as per their specific contemporary needs.

The beginning of urbanization in Kumaun Himalaya was slow but in terms of tourist destinations towns were developed and flourished as populous centers of activity. Rapid urbanization was a prominent feature of the twentieth century in the entire Kumaun Himalayan region. From the historical view point some part of Kumaun remained relatively unexplored till discoved by the British. Undoubtedly the British have contributed significantly towards urbanization in Kumaun, they established new settlements and many administrative centers after they occupied the territory of Kumaun in 1816, after the treaty of Sigauli. Systematic enumeration started in the 19th century, before this the history of urbanization is not authentic because of the lack of reliable records. The developments of roads, railways, agriculture, commerce, education and other infrastructural facilities resulted in the speedy urbanization in the region.

The process of urbanization in Nainital was a complex

phenomenon that is affected by the physical, cultural, social, religious and economic structure of the region. In Lesser Himalayas most the habitat centers were developed, particularly in the Kumaun region, owing to its unique physico-cultural and economic conditions, the process of urbanization was slower than most of other regions of the country. Not only their numbers but also the size of these towns was small. Even then, they played an important role in changing and setting of the socio-economic aspects of the region. Varying altitudes, terrains, micro-climatic characteristics, accessibility, pilgrimage and beautiful landscapes have been the main factors towards the development of urban centers of Kumaun Himalaya.

Nainital is one among the towns which was developed by the Colonial Rulers, Discovered in 1841 AD as claimed by the British, Nainital was populated rapidly in the next 10 years and soon Municipal Board was established formally in the year 1850. Afterwards several rules and regulations were laid down to develop the town. First construction was the *Pilgrim Lodge* and then several other bungalows and buildings were constructed in the first decade of its exposure to the colonial rulers.

This new process had accelerated the exogenous urban scenario and revolutionised the indigenous urbanization in the Himalayan domain. Nainital was one of the important towns among the 80 resort centres developed during 1815-1947 by the Europeans in the hilly parts adjoining Delhi, Madras, Bombay and Calcutta for their leisure and delight. They all were developed in the sites experiencing mild and pleasant climate, safety and panoramic beauty. This began a part of British colonial ecosystem and was an expression of the socio-spatial organization peculiar to colonial urban development. Thus in this part of the Himalaya, the surroundings of Nainital which was inhabited in the first half of the 19th century grew into a town of 7,589 people by 1881, 39,840 by 2001 and about 50,000 persons at present as permanent residents of the town along with floating population. In addition to this, 3.5 to 4.00 lac tourists are added annually. On the basis of the Revenue Survey carried out in 1872, the total geographical area of the Nayneetal estate (as it was earlier referred to) was 16.93km^2 (26.54 sq.mile), which included settlement area 6.73 km^2 (2.60 sq mile), environs' 8.52km^2 (3.29 sq miles) and Cantonment 1.68 km^2 (0.65 sq miles) respectively. The area of the lake was reported as 0.486 km^2 (120 acre). As per records, the Nainital MB (Municipal Board) covers an area of 11.73 km^2 and the Cantonment Board possesses 2.59 km^2 areas separately. During monsoon, it gets a heavy rainfall. The monsoon rain accounts for 75% to 80% of the annual rainfall. The climate is temperate with annual rainfall generally ranging from 200-250 cm.

CLIMATE

Nainital, owing to its location, is colder than the rest of the hilly tract of Kumaun region. The neighboring areas of Almora and Ranikhet are warmer than Nainital. The monthly maximum and minimum temperatures in the town range between 32^0 C and 7^0 C. The rainy season starts earlier than in the plains and continues up to the end of September. The heaviest rainfall is observed on the outer slopes of the hills. As per the records, total average rainfall of district was 1338 mm. During winter, rains create a considerable fall in temperature. Past hundred years' precipitation data indicate the pattern of rainfall decline. The area falls under humid category. Winter rainfall and snowfall is common. Much of the forest in the watershed is of two types of evergreen Oaks, Rhododendron, Deodar,

Kafal, Cypress the in sunny and dry sites and *Moru, Uttish,* etc in moist sites with shade. The oaks are known for their massive under growth, and hence are more effective in generating ecosystem services. Amongst the more common trees and other plants are the *cypress, ash, angu, cherry-alder, various oaks, banj, rianj, tilonj, falyat, maple, rhododendron, mehal* etc. The geology of Nainital is extremely complex characterised by landslide scars and debris cover mostly associated with the Nainital Fault that separates the lake and watershed into two roughly equal parts. Already seven major landslides have occurred during the last century.

Chapter-2

Nainital: A Brief Overview

The township of Nainital lies in the 'Lake Region', which constitutes a unique geographical division on the southern terminus of the lesser Himalayan range of Nainital, is known as the Lake District of Uttarakhand due to predominance of lakes in the area. Presence of more than 60 lakes has been recorded till the 19th century. This area was known as *Parghana Chakata* or district of 60 lakes. The district boasts of some of the most scenic lakes in India. Nainital city, located at an altitude of 1,938 m is spread over an area of 11.73 km^2, of which Naini Lake covers 0.54^2 km^2. The Town of Nainital is the headquarters of Nainital Lake District and Kumaun region of Uttarakhand.

Nainital is a tourist town of international repute. Located between longitude and latitudes of 79°25´40"E.to 79°29´20"E.and 29°21´55"N to 29°24´15"N, the geography of this area constitutes the lake itself, the sharp altitudinal differences in relief, striking verticality, geological sensitivity due to proximity to the MBT, occurrence of faults and biodiversity. The lake township varies in elevation from 1406m. Lowest point at the confluence of Ballia Nala-

Krishnapur Gad and highest 2613 meters Naina Peak.The altitudinal differences of lower and upper lake levels are 1938.2 meters and 1939.5 meters respectively. The principal settlements concentrate on the slopes around the lake in all directions.

According to renowned historian Prof. Ajay S. Rawat the maximum length of the lake is 1423 meters and the maximum depth was 27.45 meters, the mean depth being 18.52 meters. The lake has a catchment area of 5.85 km^2 including Sukhatal and a surface area of 450.70^2 m^2.

A survey of the Naini Lake, conducted by the Indian Institute of Remote sensing (IIRS) in November last year, has revealed the deepest point in the lake to be 24.6 m, which is 2.85 m less than the depth of the lake established in a survey conducted in 1895 which said that the deepest region in the lake was 27.45 m.

The survey results were presented on the GIS platform for the first time and a map of the riverbed was also created. The map revealed that the shallowest part of the lake had s depth of around 4 m.

A team of scientists from IIRS, which is a unit of ISRO, had visited Nainital to conduct a bathymetry survey of the lake. Though the survey used advanced SONAL technique to map the riverbed, the earlier surveys were done physically and therefore officials said that the accuracy of the earlier surveys could not be vouched for.

The survey has revealed that most of the lake had a depth ranging between 9 and 13 m while the deepest point was mapped to be at Pashaan Devi Temple.

The scattering of several captivating beautiful lakes of various sizes in an area of roughly two hundred square kilometres has made the district of Nainital one of the most popular tourist destinations in India. Among the major lakes spotted in this part, Nainital, the crescent shaped magnificent lake with encompassing peaks, rise from 2,139 to 2,611 meters above the sea level; like a sentinel to the cup shaped densely populated valley in the Kumaun Himalaya, is the most famous. Naini Lake, the second largest lake in Lesser Himalaya, is situated in a valley running from west to east which is bound on three sides by seven high ridges and hillocks. On the north by the Naina Peak (2611 meters) and Alma Peak (2230 meters), the Lariakantha (2481 meters) and the Sher-ka-danda (2402 meters) are its eastern extremity where the ridge descends almost to the level of the lake. On the west are the rugged hills of Deopata (2434 meters), Handi Bhandi (2180 meters) and on the west Ayarpatta attains an elevation of 2352 meters diminishing gradually towards the east. On the south is the pass through where the surplus water of the lake finds an exit and forms through Balia Ravine.

Most of the old bungalows and huge buildings constructed in the early years of Settlement in Nainital by the British are in the higher locations of the ridge slopes and the later growth of habitation follows a top down pattern. In recent years it was further pushed to upper and marginal areas of the lake basin. The average slope in different areas of the watershed ranges from 19° to 32° but some hills are extremely steep, 47°-55° in parts of China peak. It drops to 1° at the Flats and in Sukhatal.

The existence of Nainital and the lake was first reported in 1841 that opened the floodgate for influx of Europeans to the lake town. The construction of buildings started in 1842 and after that land was allocated for Bazar, public utilities and Church. Soon the place became an exclusive British town and representative of modern urbanization based on provisions of civic amenities, infrastructure, formation of urban bodies responsible for framing and implementing bye-laws for urban land resource management. In 1930, the Municipal Board of Nainital laid down by-laws for regulating anthropogenic activities in fragile and geologically sensitive areas that were classified as prohibited from construction.

Amongst the hill towns in the State of Uttarakhand, Nainital occupies a unique place known for its salubrious climate and scenic beauty. The town is a popular destination and attracts thousands of tourists round the year. Nainital is an important town of the state as the High Court, Kumaun University, Uttarakhand Academy of Administration, Aryabhatta Research Institute of Observational Sciences (ARIES), Kumaun Mandal Vikas Nigam, renowned public schools such as Sherwood, All Saints' College, St. Joseph's College, St. Mary's Convent, Birla Vidya Mandir, etc. are situated here

LOCATION AND ACCESSIBILITY

Nainital is situated at a distance of 36 km. from Kathgodam, the gateway of Kumaun and the terminus of north eastern railway and 40 km from Haldwani. It is located at 304 kms from Delhi, 360 kms. from Dehradun, the state capital. The city has three entry points by road. The major entry point is via Haldwani road, the second entry point is via Bhowali road, both being at southern end of town at Tallital. The third entry point is via Kaladhungi road in the northwest of the town at Mallital. The nearest airport is at Pantnagar 71 kms in the plains.

REGIONAL SETTING

Almora district lies to the north of Nainital and to its south lies Udham Singh Nagar district. Champawat district flanks it in the east and the district of Pauri Gahwal lies in the west. The nearby places of importance includes Bhowali (11 km), Bhimtal (22 km), Naukuchiatal (26 km),

Sattal (24 km) and Khurpatal (10 km). Cradled in the Himalayan foothills, Nainital acts as the gateway to Kumaun Hills.The hill towns of Almora and Ranikhet are 62 kms and 63 kms distantce respectively. Kausani, famous for its unparalleled view of 250 km-panoramic Himalayan range is 116 Km away from Nainital. Pithoragarh which shares its boundary with Nepal, is at a distance of 131 km while the Pindari Glacier, a popular destination for mountaineers and trekkers, is 236 km away. The world famous Jim Corbett National Park is 117 km away from Nainital.

BRIEF HISTORICAL BACKGROUND

Nainital is referred to in the *Manas Khand* of the *Skanda Purana* as the *Tri-Rishi-Sarovar*, the lake of the three sages, *Atri, Pulastya* and *Pulaha* who were reputed to have arrived here on a penitential pilgrimage, and finding no water to quench their thirst, dug a hole and siphoned water into it from Mansarovar, the sacred lake in Tibet.

According to the Skanda Purana "When the earth of Mansarovar touches any one's body, or when anyone bathes in the lake, he shall go to the *Brahm Lok* (Heaven of Brahma). He who drinks its waters shall go to the *Shiva Lok* (Paradise of Shiva) and shall be released from the sins of a hundred births. Even the beast that bears the name of Mansarovar shall go to the *Brahma Lok.* Its waters are like precious pearls." Hindus believed that a dip in Nainital, 'the lesser Mansarovar', earned merit equal to a dip in the great Mansarovar Lake.

This place was considered so sacred, that the snake God, Nag *Karkotak,* ordained that in the vicinity of Nainital, snake bite should not result in death. It is not surprising that before the advent of the British the whole valley of Nainital was treated as a temple by the Hindus and people entered the valley after bathing and removing their footwear in reverence.

The second important mythological reference to Nainital is as one of the 64 *Shakti Peeths,* i.e. centres of powers of the Shakti cult. These centres were created wherever parts of the body of Sati fell, when Lord Shiva was carrying around her corpse in grief. It is said that the left eye (*Nayan*) of Sati fell here, and this gave rise to the patron deity of the town 'Nainital', the lake of the eye. The Nainital lake does resemble an eye and one can understand why the ancient thought of it as the eye of the Goddess, fallen here from the shoulders of the great Shiva himself.

Sati was the consort of Lord Shiva, her father *Dakshaprajapati* deliberately insulted Lord Shiva by not inviting him to a grand *yagya* held at Kankhal, near Haridwar. Shocked by her father's behaviour and unable to bear the insult to her divine husband, Sati immolated herself in the sacred fire.

Shiva then shouldered the corpse of Sati in grief and began roving frantically owing to which the balance of the universe was disturbed. Lord Vishnu the Preserver then intervened and released his *Sudarshan Chakra,* the celestial disc, ensuring that every part of the body of Sati was cut off. When no portion of her corpse was left, only then Lord Shiva was released from the spell of grief. Every place where a part of the body fell, gave rise to a deity, and is considered a *Shakti Peeth.* According to a legend, the left eye (*Nayan*) of Sati dropped in the lake while her body was being carried by Lord Shiva to Kailash Parvat. Hence, the lake was given the name of *Nayneetal,* from where the city derives its name. Naina Devi is worshipped as the patron deity of the town. Naina Devi temple is located at the northern end of the lake. The temple was destroyed in the landslide which occurred in 1880. It was subsequently replaced by the present structure.

In the year 1841, Mr. P. Barron an enthusiastic European merchant from Rosa, near Shahjahanpur took great fancy to this land. It is relatively lesser known that this region was called "Khasdesh" in ancient times and "Khas" ruled this region before Christ was born.

Nainital had become a popular hill resort by 1847. The Nainital Municipal Board was formally constituted in 1845. It was the second Municipal Board of the North-Western Provinces. In 1862, Nainital became the summer seat of the North Western Provinces. The town also became the summer seat of the U.P. Government after independence. After 1963, the summer exodus of the U.P. Government was stopped. The Secretariat building is now being used by the High Court of Uttarakhand.

SIGNIFICANCE OF URBAN SITE

Towns grow and develop at different sites for discharging specific functions. The development of urban centers was purposesd in the Lake Region because of its salubrious climate, picturesque surrounding and beauty of lakes. There are many urban centers in this region, and Nainital is one of them. The town encompasses the area around Naini Lake, combined with bracing climate and proximity to the densely populated plains of North India as well as being the administrative headquarters of the Nainital district in the Kumaun division of Uttarakhand; it is an important town in the region and one of the most popular tourist destinations.

NAINITAL: GEOGRAPHICAL INTRODUCTION

Nainital is the main urban centre of the region situated in the Lesser Himalaya near the MBT. The lake in the center of this town is an unusual natural phenomenon; no other lake of the many other found in this region can be compared

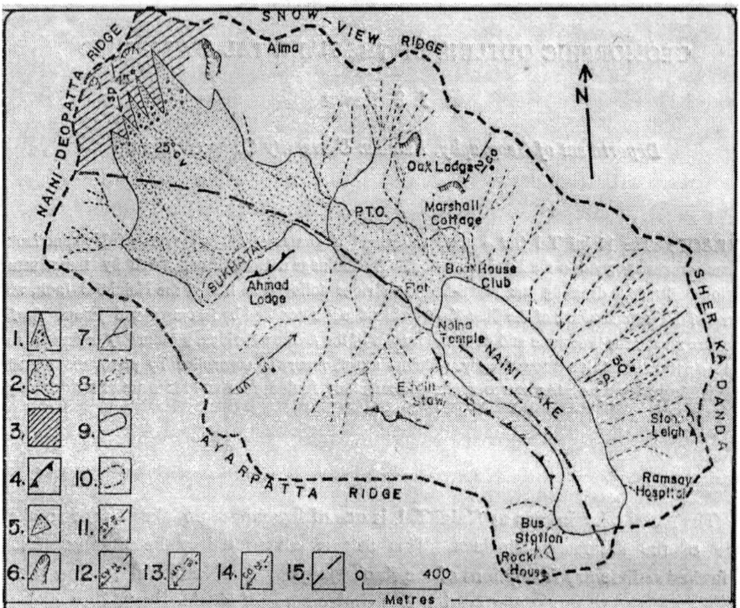

igure 1. Geomorphological map of the Naini lake basin. References : (1) Debris cone, (2) Landslide deposits, (3) Free face, (4) Scarp, (5) Triangular fault facet, (6) Landslide scar, (7) Perennial stream, (8) Seasonal stream, (9) Lake, (10) Dry lake bed, (11) straight planar slope of 45°, (12) Concave slope of 25°, (13) Undulating slope of 18°, (14) Convex slope of 21°, (15) Naini Tal fault.

After J.S.Rawat (1988):Geomorphic outline of Nainital watershed, Geographic Review of India, Vol.50, No.1, pp.53-62.

with the eye shaped lake, an outcome of tectonic activities.

Geographically the district is divided into two zones viz. Hilly and Bhabar. The hilly region in outer Himalayas is known to geologist as Krol. The foothill area of the district is known as Bhabhar. The name Bhabhar is derived from a tall growing grass growing in the region. The underground water level is very deep in this region. The hilly region of the district has many lakes. *Nainital, Bhimtal, Sattal, Naukuchiatal, Khurpatal, Harishtal, Lokhamtal,* etc. are known bigger lakes of the district.

ORIGIN OF LAKE IN GEOLOGICAL THEORY

The origin of Lake Nainital and the other lakes of Kumaun have always been a subject of controversy. There are two main theories, first that it was excavated by the glacial action and was formed by a landslide. Some have suggested that the valley had been dammed up by landslide debris.

In Nainital hills, in the southern fringe of the Kumaun Himalaya from a prominent physiographic feature characterized by a complex tectonic architecture related to boundary thrust and recurrent movements along faults, structurally one of the most disturbed belts of the Himalayas, this massif is a product of movements on the Intra-plate Subduction Zone - The Main Boundary Thrust.

Different opinions, regarding the origin of the lakes, given by different geologist are:

(i) Theobold (1880) thought that the stream channel was blocked by a glacial moraine.

(ii) Middlemiss (1890), Heim and Ganseer (1939), Thomas (1952), Pande (1974) and Valdiya (1981) invoke differential movements along a fault to explain formation of the lake depression. Middlemiss believed in different movement along a fault accompanied by the enlargement of cavities of the collapsed mass of limestone.

(iii) Thomas postulated gliding down of the southern Ayarpatta block on plastic red-shale horizon and development of a charm behind the glided block.

(iv) Mathur (1955) described the lake as structural valley that has been enlarged by denudation of their floors.

(v) Pal and Merch (1974) see the Nainital Lake as a product of a combined effect of movements along intersecting Nainital, Khurpatal and Lariakanta fault - the subsidence of the nose of the synclinal hills.

(vi) Hukku*et al.* (1974) think that the Naini and Khurpa lakes represent remnant loops of meandering river that vanished as a result of neotectonic movements along the active Manora Thrust. What Hukku described as fluvioglacial deposits are indeed blocking upper Krol collapsed down between parallel faults.

Chapter-3

Historical Sketch of Urbanisation in Nainital

In the *Manaskhand* of *Skanda Purana,* the present township Nainital was known as 'Tri Rishi Sarovar' but some historical facts about this place apprise of the movements of pilgrims on the way to famous *Dhams* of Uttarakhand. The place was designated 'Naynee Tal 'or 'Nainital' to the local people due to the existence of a deified lake and a sacred temple of goddess *Nayna Devi.* The Kumaun region was under Gorkha rule from 1790 to 1815. It was acceded to British rule in 1815. Nainital was an unpopulated forested area with Naina Devi temple at Mallital and known only to local natives.

It is an accepted fact that after the British occupation, G.W. Traill (815-1835), the second Commissioner of Kumaun was the first British to visit this enchanting valley. In 1841, a young European from Roza Wine Factory, Shahjahanpur, having some pre information about the wilderness and beauty of the area, presence of a beautiful lake and a vision to establish a resort, finally succeeded in locating Nainital with the help of a local guide. He describes his journey to discover the land beyond his imagination in the following way. ***"It would take a month to explore the*** *magnificent scenery around Nainital. It is by far the most beautiful site I have witnessed in the course of a fifteen hundred miles trek in the Himalaya."*

Barren popularized his discovery through the newspapers. In 1841 an issue of the *'Calcutta Englishman'* published the news titled ***"The discovery of a lake in the vicinity of Almora"***. A subsequent description of Nainital and its environs in the ***Agra Akhbar*** appeared as ***"The lake is situated on the range of mountains overhanging the plains, called the Gagar, and is distant about 35 miles from Almora...It is slightly curved in shape, about 1¼ to 1½ miles in length, and its greatest breadth, I should say, about three quarters of a mile...the water is as clear as crystal, a beautiful little stream supplied from the springs of the overtopping mountains, is continually running into it, and a smaller one flowing out of it, at the opposite extremity. An undulating lawn, with a great deal of level ground, interspersed with occasional clumps of oak, cypress and other beautiful trees, continues from the margin of the lake, for upward of a mile up to the base of a magnificent mountain standing at the further extreme of this vast amphitheatre; and the sides of the lake are also bounded by splendid hills and peaks, which are thickly wooded down to the water's edge. On the undulating ground between the highest level and the margin of the lake, there are capabilities for a race -course, cricket ground etc. and building sites in every direction for a large town."***

His next visit was a year later in December 1842. The place had not remained in its former obscurity. About half a dozen sites had already either been applied for or granted, and Mr. George Thomas Lushington, the then Commissioner of Kumaun, had started to build a small house. Moreover, the Commissioner had already planned out a bazaar on the site of the present Mallital. This rapid development of Nainital was apparently welcome to the people, who according to Barron, *"were flocking in to take leases of land for shops"*. Barron himself selected three sites. In 1842, he constructed a house for himself, *Pilgrim Lodge*, just above the present Nainital Club. Barron had brought with him from the plains, a boat measuring about 6 m in length. After some difficulty it reached Nainital safely, the day after his arrival, he and his friends launched it on the lake, and went for a row. This discovery as a historic event laid down the foundation of a new township.

Evolution of The Township and Early Urban Development

As stated earlier the township is comparatively a very recent origin. The crescent shape lake is the principal attraction around which has evolved the town and its entire morphology. The picturesque surroundings, together with the beauty of the lake, its proximity to the plains and a salubrious climate, not unlike that of England were the main reasons that led to the selection of Nainital as a recreation and health resort by the British. The motive was also to establish a site for their cultural, administrative and political requirements. When Barron came to Nainital again in November 1843, the urbanization was well advanced. It was like a birth of a new child. According to the earliest data available on tourists in Nainital, it had become a popular hill resort by 1847. In the same year the Commissioner of Kumaun reported to the Government that 40 houses had been built at Nainital and two were in the course of construction. Twenty-six casual visitors had come to the place between March and August 1847 and sixty-one had spent the summer season in Nainital. An Octroi Board initially formed in 1845 and finally Municipal Board was constituted in1850; it was the second Municipal Board of the North Western Provinces, even before the concerned act became operative in the then United Provinces. To catalyze the formation of a town, the administration transferred tracts of land, particularly to the wealthy Sah community of Almora, on condition that they will construct the houses on the land.

Nainital assumed a new importance in 1857. There was no outbreak of disorder here and it played an important role as a place of security for the refugees from the neighboring plains stations. In 1860 Nainital became the summer seat of the North Western Provinces. After it was made the summer capital, a remarkable expansion of the town occurred with the growth of magnificent bungalows all around and construction of facilities such as marketing areas, rest houses, the secretariat and other administrative units. It also became an important centre of education for the British.

During the middle of the 19th century, the place witnessed a phenomenal rise in many urban functions and various institutional and non-institutional facilities and socio-economic services emerged to serve the growing needs of the town. In 1860, Nainital was made the *Summer Capital* of N.W. Provinces in 1862 and this was followed by the remarkable expansion of the township and its status. Gradually the town expends and the population recorded in 1881 census was 7589.

The catchment also hosts a large floating population of about 5000 people during the peak tourist season who were mostly workers as such as petty vendors, coolies, boatmen, horsemen, etc. Nainital registered a gradual increase in its population size. The opening of the rail link up to Haldwani and Kathgodam in 1882 and 1899 and the creation of a new *Nainital District* with the establishment of head quarter, were among the significant factors that helped in the early growth of the town. An immense growth in population, 48.8%, uras recorded in the first decade of the new millennium.

Urban Growth

Demographic Profile

The behavior of decadal growth rate of population of Nainital-Municipal area has been erratic, varying in a wide range. The growth rates in some years, both positive and negative are incredible.

The population and growth of the town is shown in the table.

Conspicuously, the decadal growth rate of 43% in 1901 - 11 dropped to 10 % low in the following decade. Still

Census Year	Nainital M B		Nainital Cantt		Nainital UA	
	Population	*Dcadal Growth %*	*Population*	*Dcadal Growth %*	*Population*	*Dcadal Growth %*
1881	7589	-	-	-	7589	-
1891	8455	-	-	-	8455	-
1901	6903	-	-	-	6903	-
1911	10270	48.76	-	-	10270	-
1921	11230	935	-		11230	-
1931	9741	-13.26	932	37.88	10673	-
1941	9539	-2.07	539	28.32	10116	-
1951	12350	29.47	743	46.03	13093	-
1961	14995	21.42	1085	46.03	16080	22.81
1971	23986	59.96	1181	8.85	25167	56.51
1981	24835	3.54	1258	6.52	26093	3.68
1991	29837	20.14	1144	11.45	30951	18.62
2001	38559	29.23	1281	11.97	39840	28.72

Source: *Census of India, 1991-series 25 UP PartIX-A. & Census of India 2001, Table-03.*

more conspicuous, as the Table indicates, is that Nainital had negative growth rate in the decade 1921-31 (- 9%), and no growth at all (0%) in the decade 1931-41. This phenomenon gives a clear indication that during these two decades there had been a large exodus of population from the town. For, even the natural growth of population in the 1931 decade was overtaken by the rate of out-migration, and in the decade of 1941 was evened out by the rate of population exodus from the town. This situation was not repeated in the later decades but the trend of growth rate has not been smooth.

The decades of 1961-71 and 1971-81 witnesses some big surprises. While in the former decade the decadal growth rate shot up to as high as 71%, in the later decade it recorded a 4% low. By implication, 4% decadal growth rate (i.e. less than 0.5 % per annum) being much lower than even the natural growth rate of population in India. It may be inferred that in this decade also, Nainital was de-populated. In the decade 1981-91 the growth rate shot up to 20%, and in 1991-2001 decade, it recorded 26.67%, exceeding the national average of 21.53% for the same decade.

The population however, not records any significant increase during the four decade of the century after 1911 and result in only 13093 in comparison to count of 1951. This phenomenon can be elaborated with the fact that in the 1931 census, Nainital cantonment was considered separate. Establishment of a cantonment as a separate entity contributed to the decline of population of the Nainital Municipal Board. The decline of population was also related to the *Lee Commission Free Passage Scheme (LCFPS)* which permitted a large number of British army and civil officers to take leave and send their families home in summer after independence. In 1960, the state government decided not to continue the shift of summer capital to Nainital. Initially this step proved a damaging factor for the growth and status of the town along with the economy of the town.

During the years, therefore, there has been an increase in the built up area of the town mainly in the form of the tourist facilities along with the mall road. At the two ends of the lake there are congested markets with multi-storeyed old houses. The surrounding ridges constitute the residential units, although such houses are also found in the lower adjoining areas near the lake. Correspondingly, there has been a significant increase in the anthropogenic pressure owing to 'expansion 'and 'aggregation' aspects of the urbanization process.

There is no doubt that man has been the most active agent in shaping the face of his own habitat during the course of the historical development, but it is the nature of the earth, which also determines the pattern of its future growth. The location of any human settlement and its growth depends upon the interplay of various natural and cultural factors ranging over a period of time. This phenomenon can be seen through the settlement and growth of Nainital town. The picturesque surrounding, together with the beauty of the lake, its proximity to the plains and salubrious climate were the main reasons that led to the selection of Nainital as a recreationd and health resort by the British during the nineteenth century.

Prior to 1839, little historical records of Nainital were available; however, villagers knew the place as it had a religious significance for them. The first recorded account of Nainital is found in an issue of the newspaper "Englishman from Calcutta" which was followed by a letter of Peter Barron published in *Agra Akhabar* in 1841. Mr. G.W. Trail, the second Commissioner visited Nainital while conducting revenue settlements of Kumaun in 1817, but he did not pay much interest to this area. P. Barron (nick named as Pilgrim) popularized this wilderness to the outside world, mentions that the whole area was covered with dense forest only frequented by locals of surrounding villages, who visited the place with their cattle during the summer and rainy seasons to use abundant pasture of the valley.

P.Barron reached Nainital on 18 November 1841 through Khairna, Kafulta, Jakh, Chaursa, St. Loo Gorge. Before 1841, there was hardly even a hut in the valley but by 1842 about half a dozen sites for buildings had been applied for and granted. After returning from Nainital almost after two months Peter Barren sent an application from Shahjahanpur to Senior Assistant Commissioner J.H. Batting to build a house and garden at Nainital on Lease. Barren was the first European, who applied for a land in Nainital. Batting replied in his letter and mentioned that Commissioner Kumaun Mr. G.T. Lushington will look into the matter after a proper inspection of the site and formulate rules for the allocation of land. Secretary board of revenue North-West Province H.M. Eliot, ordered Commissioner Kumaun to finalize the rules and regulations for the allocation of land in Nainital. The Commissioner was authorized to exercise all rights to declare any area as a public property for common use. A small bazaar and houses for businessmen were planned out and areas were demarcated near the upper end of the lake. Barron selected three sites for him, and constructed a house named 'Pilgrim Lodge'.

G.T. Lushington, the then Commissioner of Kumaun, also applied for a piece of land in Nainital. Commissioner Lushington, Peter Barren, G.B. Sanders (Neighbor of Barren in Shahjanpur), Mr. Mclayell, Dr. Kolkohan were the pioneering applicants for applying land in Nainital. In 1842 the Government of North-West Province (NWP) decided to conduct revenue settlement in Nainital. Secretary Board of Revenue North-West Province H.M. Eliot wrote a letter on 21st October 1842 to Secretary of N.W. Province N.C. Hamalton regarding the land on the sides of the lake and this land was under the control of NWP government. After taking permission of NWP Government *two aana per kacchabigha* rate was finalized for the land and, the amount generated from this lease rent was decided to deposit for the betterment and development of Nainital. Secretary North-West Province H.B. Riddel wrote a letter to H.M. Eliot on 3rd December 1842 regarding the consent of Governor General for issuing land lease at Nainital. A further order issued to the Board of Revenue, allocation of suitable good land shall be left for market place, fairs, public buildings, parks, churches, etc. Board of Revenue was further asked to seek permission from Lt. Governor to appoint any officer for survey of Nainital.

In 1843 Peter Barren celebrated Christmas at his under construction Bungalow 'Pilgrim Lodge'. Till December of 1843 not a single house was constructed completely. However construction of some boats was ongoing on near the lake in 1943. In this duration any British who wanted to construct a house in Nainital, used to mark a sign in the trees of his favorite site. It was considered an offense to erase remove those marks on the trees of that reserved site. One has to submit an application with full details of land for development; construction work Was permitted only after sanction of lease by the authorities.

In the year 1845, it was decided that Nainital should have a local self government and to foremost this on 8th May 1845, nearly around 10 households of Nainital sent a proposal to the Governor to establish a Municipal Board at

Nainital under the Act X of 1842.

The rapid expansion of the township soon received the attention of Commissioner Lushington and compelled him to ban private lease, as he wanted to conserve some land for public amenities like post office, hospital, school and police station, etc. With the gradual expansion of the settlements and population, the need of a local self-government was felt, and on the request of local citizens, in 1845, the By Laws Act No. X of Bengal Presidency was implemented in the town. As a result, a committee was setup to give priority to develop essential infrastructure in the town and also pass a resolution to clean the lake and remove algae from it. Soon doctors and policemen were also deployed in the town.

This Municipal Act X of 1842 was issued for Bengal Province only, therefore the proposal was not considered by the British Government although the denizens of the town constituted a Municipal Board Committee for Nainital. Major General Sir W. Richards, Maj. George Lushington, Maj. H.H. Arnold, Capt. W.P. Wang and Mr. P. Barren were the members of the committee. It was a herculean task for the committee to urbanize Nainital as a planned and an ideal town. This committee had a long list of proposed tasks for future development of the town. One of the main problems to achieve the targets was the lack of human resource as well as other resources for the development. One of the major problem was that there were no roads as well as connecting paths in the town, light and cleaning also need to be handled. A taxation plan and management of income was essential potable water for the town was urgently required. Overall, a new town has to be carved out from the dense forest and to achieve these a set of effective rule has to be formulated under existing geographical and ecological conditions. The committee had a vision, to create a town which could provide similar feeling as of any town of England. The Committee not only accepted the challenges but they succeeded in shaping the town as per their plan. With the help of the local administration of Municipal Board, the committee focused on a system of transportation and priority was given to Nainital-Kaladhungi road. To meet requirement, for labours in 1845, a Coolie Jamadar was appointed and he was granted a title of 'Superintendent of Coolies'.

Lala Moti Ram Sah from Almora played a pivotal role in the process of urbanization of Nainital. General W. Richard's was influenced by the personality of Lala Moti Ram Sah, he appointed him as a Government Cashier. British Government invited prosperous Sah families from Almora for the settlement of Nainital and allocated them land with the condition that they will construct their own house at the earliest, as suggested by Lala Moti Ram Sah. In 1845 the site of the Mallital market area prepared for settlement purpose, before that it was covered with a thick *ringal* bamboo forest. The present Mallital Bazaar was earlier occupied with thick (bamboo) and other trees, where wild animals like Tiger, Leopard, Sambhar, etc. wander around. In later phase of the 1845, construction of houses as well as shops at Mallital Bazaar were initiated. In the year 1846, the market in this area was developed and there was an increase in the number of new buildings in Mallital Bazaar.

In the year 1845, the district Post Office was opened and the distribution of the posts of government department begins. A runner carries government posts from one post office to another.

In 1846 the construction of Nainital-Kaladhungi road was started and this year sweepers were brought from

Moradabad for the purpose of maintaining cleanliness in the town. In 1847, the construction of roads in the periphery of lake the started and a site was selected for the Church St. John's in the Wilderness on the edge of Mallital Bazaar, St. John in the Wilderness is one of the earliest building erected in the town and one of the finest in the region, the church was named by the Bishop of Calcutta who visited Nainital in the year 1844.

In 1847 six police men were deputed at Nainital and the Nainital-Khairna road construction had also started. In the same year a flats (ground) was developed, as there was paucity of labors for developmental work, so that the prisoners were used to develop the ground.

Till 1847, Nainital become a popular hill station and the result, tourist started visiting here. Till year 1847, a total 40 houses were constructed completely and several under construction. There is one interesting fact that the earlier house owners of Nainital were close friends of Peter Barren. It was mandatory for the house owners that they will not harm any trees during the construction and if such happens, then the owner needs to plant more than of total damaged trees. This order is an eye opener for the present scenario of Nainital, and shows that the British were very concerned for the town and its ecology. Now days many of the houses have been constructed after lopping, damaging and falling of several trees and no new plantation has been carried out. In 1848 another road from Nihal Bridge to Khurpatal was started it was constructed in a record time and the road which was started in 1847 in the periphery of lake was also completed in the record one year. This is the work culture that we need to learn from the British that how to complete the task within the stipulated time frame and with the limited resources. Today in the 21st Century we cannot imagine construction of the road around the lake with in a limited period of one year.

By the year 1847, forty houses were constructed in Nainital and 61 visitors enjoyed their summers and 26 other people visited Nainital. The town becames famous in a short span of a time. In a decade only there was a remarkable growth of settlements, which resulted in acquiring the status of a Municipality in 1850.

In 1850, Industrialization began in India and the government passed a Municipal Act - XXVI which covered the entire country. As this act was applied on 3rd October 1850, the Nainital Municipal Committee was notified legally. Nainital Municipal Committee had a glory to be the second Municipal Board of North West Provinces. New members needed to be nominated for the committee, out of that one Senior Deputy Commissioner, District Engineer, and three other high officials were designated. Senior Deputy Commissioner was the Chairman of the Committee and the Assistant Commissioner Nainital was given the responsibility to be the Vice-Chairman as well as the Secretary of the Municipal Board. The pace of development was accelerated after receiving a statutory status of the Nainital Municipal Board. In the year 1851 the total income of Municipal Board of Nainital was Rupees 2300/- and Rs. 1000 approximate was the expenditure on the construction of roads.

To protect the town from congestion and to maintain the beauty and integrity of the landscape, it was made mandatory that each bungalow shall be surrounded by at least two acres of natural forests. By 1850, Nainital became a well known hill station and attracted herds of tourists. A regular arrival of people required a systematic development of the township and provision for various amenities like roads, parks, grounds, offices and schools etc. In order to serve the growing needs of the people, a town required many facilities and a number of services. A mission school was set-up in 1850 which was later named as Chet Ram Sah Thulgharia School in 1928, and it is considered the first school of the town. In 1851, the Collectorate building was constructed and a police station was also opened in the town.

During the monsoon season, the Sukhatal Lake was filled with fresh water and it was known as Malla Pokhar and Nainital was known as Talla Pokhar. In the summers the Sukhatal Lake was used as a shooting range. In 1855, activities of Forest Department started in Nainital for the better management of its forests, and in the year 1855 Nainital was declared as a head quarter for Kumaun Zone. In 1856, one of the most popular British Administrator, Maj. General Sir Henry Ramsey was appointed as the Commissioner of Kumaun and he was given an additional charge of Forest Conservator. The office of Forest Conservator was also opened in Nainital and Henry Ramsey becomes the first Forest Conservator in Northern India. In 1858 Messer's Davis established an Iron Company named Kumaon Iron Company and 3 lime kilns were also constructed near Bara Patthar. Iron from these kilns was the main source of construction of strong buildings at Nainital.

During the first war of Indian Independence the British sought a safe refuge in Nainital and considered this place to be ideal for safeguarding their families in terms of both safety and climate. In the summers season, most of the British used to visit Shimla but now they found another beautiful town which could provide then a safe refuge also. In 1862, Nainital was declared as a summer capital of North-Western Provinces. A bungalow was acquired for Lt. Governor at Stoneleigh area, subsequently many government offices were shifted to Nainital as per requirement of the functioning of summer capital. In earlier phase, the offices were scattered but soon after the number of employees was increased henceforth, Pavilion house was also acquired for the Secretariat. Every year on1st November the Secretariat was again resifted to Agra as on annual basis. As Nainital become summer capital of the North-Western Provinces, the development process of Nainital accelerated, construction work was increased and many houses were constructed for the purpose of rent. There was a rapid increase in the population of Nainital during that period, there was an increase in the business too and the town becames more popular. An assembly room was also constructed near the lake for the meetings of the Municipal Board, parties, dance and theatre activities.

In the opinion of Prof. Ajay S. Rawat, Nainital assumed a new importance in 1857. There was no outbreak of disorder here and it played an important role as a place of security for the refugees from the neighboring plains stations.

In 1857, Nainital becomes a safe refuge as a minor impact of mutiny was felt here, when the country was witnessing the outbreak of violence and disorder. It was considered to be a safe haven for Europeans. Soon it becomes a significant centre of education for Europeans. Nainital Diocesan, the present Sherwood College, was opened in July 1867 to provide schooling to both European boys and girls. A new school was opened in 1869 for the education of European girls with the name All Saints' Sisters. A few more schools, the Oak Opening Boys High School (in 1877) later renamed as Philander Smith School afterward Hallet War School and presently as Birla Vidya Mandir and St. Mary's Convent (1878) was also opened. Wellesley College was another premier institute of India during the colonial period; today the D.S.B. Campus (1951), the main campus of the Kumaun University is located. Hotel

Mayo, which was renamed Grand Hotel in 1898 was the first hotel of the town, which was built in 1870.

In the first 25 years of its habitation, Nainital was developed into a beautiful and well managed town. (1857 onwards a cantonment area, named Gorkha Line was also developed for an army establishment in Nainital.) In 1867 a formal estate plan was completed after measuring and mapping Nainital through scientific methods and authenticated maps of estates were prepared. It was considered as a primary formal and authentic survey of Nainital. Up to 1867, including the Tallital and Mallital market total 169 governments and private estates were constructed and a total of 815 acres (approx.) land was distributed for this purpose. (Annexure-I)

Nainital is situated in a very sensitive geological area as this is clearly brought out by the geo-tectonic disturbances, and some minor or major landslides that occur every now and then. Nainital as seen by Pilgrim earlier had no fresh landslides, mainly because it was free from human pressure. However, records refer to several incidents of land slips, boulders rolling or washing away of roads even in the years passed. Actually the fragility of the ecosystem could not be visualized in advance.

The British government was busy in the expansion of infrastructure and facilities in Nainital and suddenly the town experienced first serious environmental hazard related to hill slopes in 1867, which manifested in a massive landslide, when a huge landmass of Alma Hill, near the Mallital Bazaar, came down. In the year 1867 just after 25 years of its habitation, a landslide was occurred in Popular Estate at Mallital. In this landslide a newly constructed cottage of Victoria Hotel was truckled down in the debris and one Indian citizen died because of landslide, after the incident an inquiry committee was setup immediately. In

1873 a committee was framed under the Chairmanship of Col. Brownlow, in its report the committee suggested to make necessary arrangement the drain out the rain water properly and to adopt measures for percolation of water the inquiry committee suggested that construction of safety walls and drains is compulsorily required for the safety of the hill. This calamity worried the local administration, soon a committee was constituted to consider the matter of safety of the hill slopes. The area was declared sensitive and the sale and purchase of land was banned in some of the fragile areas. The committee in its inquiry found that no drainage system exists in Nainital catchment and suggested it as one of the most important safety measures for preventing further landslides. In 1869 again the Popular Estate faced a fresh landslide but this time no damage and loss of life was recorded, but the British took it seriously and a scientific method was included in conservation and development for better health services. In 1869 a Medical College was also opened and 8 males and 4 females were given basic training of medical sciences.

Nainital was developed by the British with a specific vision of perfect planning which be visible in the schemes of bungalows. The bungalows of British officer were constructed representing the hierarchy as per the height of hill, grandeur and aristocracy. The aristocratic segment mentioned a distance from lower class, for this purpose, the highest peak of the hill was selected for the construction of bungalows. Bungalows for Senior British Officials like Lt. Governor, Army Commanders, and other high officials were constructed according to the height of hill so that they can impose their supremacy along with to adore the natural beauty of the lake and valley from the top of the hill.

In the basic concept of urbanization and habitation

pattern of Nainital, it is clearly visible that there is a sense of superior race and highness of the British. The British initially planed to urbanize Nainital for prosperous and high class people and initially there was a system to allocate 7 acres of land to an applicant so that they can build a large bungalow. Senior additional Commissioner Nainital was authorized to allocate the land. On 8th December 1869 land tax was increased from 12 *aana* per acre to 2 rupees per acre.

Colonial rulers developed a new style of architecture for the town. In this architectural style a bungalow was constructed with the locally available resources, designed according to the climate, and use of local labors with British engineers. This blended conglomerate free style architecture was popularly known as 'Nainital Pattern'. However Gothic style of architecture was followed for the churches and public buildings of Nainital. In the blended architectural style bungalows were constructed with a loft above a double story, kitchen constructed on a certain distance from the main building and both the buildings were connected through the arch-way. A small house was also constructed with a distance from the main bungalow which was known as 'sunny side' or 'glass house'. Next to a bungalow a tennis court was also planned and the bungalow was surrounded with gardens and a kitchen garden. In the corner of the bungalow site, a small servant's quarters was also constructed which was known as 'Out House'. A Stable and *Dandi* (Palanquin) shade was also constructed in the premises. One small house was also there for the washer man. It was necessary for the bungalow owner to make arrangement for all their needs along with their servants. Most of the population of the town was residing in these Out Houses.

A bungalow owner had the responsibility of cleaning

his campus and to channelized rain water in the nearest public drains. It can be made out very clearly that only a resourceful person could construct bungalows here and was are capable to create and maintain the above mentioned infrastructure, otherwise the only option was to take a house on rent or to stay in a hotel.

Like other hill stations, Nainital was one of the favorite places of the British. Nainital was known for being center the of academics and rest and recoup. During the Colonial period the British consider at Nainital as a part of England due to its salubrious climate and it was termed as 'Choti Vilayat'. The numbers of applications were increasing day by day for construction of Bungalows in Nainital, so it was not possible to allocate 7 acre, land for everyone, to face this problem in 1877 a new rule was formulated and it was known as '4 acre rule. According to this rule 4 acre of land was allocated to construct a bungalow, so that the environment and ecology of Nainital shall remain protected and this will prevent the town to be over populated.

The Mallital area of the town is comparatively plain and favorable for construction, In the initial years most of the bungalows were constructed in Mallital area. Pilgrim Lodge, Nainital Club, Vilayathe Cottage, Sunny Site, Cyprus Cottage were constructed before the year 1872. Amongst the Hotels Mayo, Belvedere, Metropole, Royal, Swiss and Weldroff were constructed in the early years.

Till 1880, Nainital became a prosperous town with the all available facilities, on 17 September 1880, the population of Nainital was10054 with 2957 females and 7097 males. The British were happy in the climate and the rejuvenating weather of Nainital. The fragile system of the town could not be safeguarded for a long time and on 18th September 1880 Nainital again witnessed the most devastating landslides of the century. Before that, some small landslide occurred and the British were aware of the sensitivity of Bray Side Hill and a drainage system was developed on the 'Darjeeling pattern'. However the 'Darjeeling pattern' of drainage system was proved to be an unsuccessful attempt here. Due to heavy rainfall, construction of bungalows, gardens, tennis courts, road construction, falling of green trees, etc., the ecology and natural system of Nainital was disturbed. Owing to construction, in the natural slope of rain water channels were blocked and because of constructions, natural drains were disturbed, that created a problem of water drainage from bungalows and other sites. Hilly tracts were leveled so that the water could not enter the hill slopes through the cracks. Excess underground water could not found the proper way and the carrying capacity of hill slopes was feeble. This condition was triggered by a small tremor and the water blocked within the slope of Sher-ka-Danda Hill slided down and big chunk of hill moved towards the lake. The immediate cause of the land slide was a slight earthquake on the fatal day of 18th September, together with 50.8 cm. to 63.5 cm. of heavy rain prior to the land slide. This land slide devastated Victoria Hotel, Bell shop, Naina Devi Temple, and a part of assembly room. In few seconds, geographical map of Nainital was changed.

One of the most sunny and suitable area of the town for residential purpose was washed away and taking the lives of 151 people, 43 Europeans and 108 Indians. The impact of the destruction made people alert about their town's safety. The main causes of the landslide were the lack of drainage system, digging of fresh building sites on the ridge of the hill together with the cutting of the hill side for gardens, roads and tennis courts and destruction of the grassy cover that permitted the rain water to enter into the hill side. During the relief work, Kumaun Commissioner

Sir Henry Ramsey also drowned in the rubble. After this land slide, members of the Municipal Committee resigned on the moral grounds, soon the government nominated a new members. After this disaster the colonial government became more sensitive. Serious efforts were made to understand the geology of the town and special attention was paid towards the conservation and stability of the hill slopes. Safe and unsafe areas were demarcated clearly. Under the chairmanship of Henry Ramsay a special committee was constituted and a special fund was releases to deal with the environmental problems.

Ramsay Committee was formed on 22 September 1880. Its president was Sir Henry Ramsay, the then Commissioner of Kumaun. The Ramsay Committee recommended the following measures:

i. Ravines to be lined and riveted.
ii. Fissures or long deep cracks to be filled with clay.
iii. Platforms, tennis courts and terraces to be covered with 15.24 cm. of rammed clay
iv. Further erection of buildings, quarrying and excavation of terraces or platforms to be absolutely prohibited on the affected hill side. Special care should be taken to prevent injury from house drainage. All houses to have cave gutters and masonry drains leading to the nearest suitable ravine where provision should be made for its reception.
v. Steep slopes to be planted with trees. No grass cutting or grazing to be allowed.
vi. An honest, efficient and trustworthy officer should be appointed as the Inspector of Buildings and Drains who should work under the sole orders and responsibility of the civil officer in-charge of the station.

A committee was further appointed in 1882 to consider the stability of hill slopes in and around Nainital on the request of the people to prevent a recurrence of the catastrophe of 1880. In spite of the loss of life and property, the landslide had some beneficial effects. The landslide of 1880 had one very important beneficial effect. The tragedy which occurred made the authorities thinks of the urgent need of a proper drainage system. Before the year 1880, there was practically no drainage system in Nainital, but between 1880 and 1885 a network of 29 nallahs (drains), about 71 km in length was developed. Creation of the playground Flats, as it now exists another beneficial effect of the 1880 landslide. A small recreation ground had existed there before the landslide, but as a result of it, the space available was largely increased. The Flats have become the throbbing heart of the town and is buzzing with activities. By the turn of the century Nainital became a well-known hill station and administrative center. With its growth as a hill station, tourism became an affluent business and some of the Europeans started renting their properties during the tourist season. It finally led to growth of the hotel industry.

The drainage system in Nainital was introduced by Sir Henry Ramsay after the diabolic land slide of 1880 and Rs. 3 lakhs were spent in the construction of nallahs. Accordingly, the drainage schemes to drain water from the hill slopes around Naini lake were implemented. Nallahs, 79 km in length were constructed throughout the hill slopes of Nainital next year's. These nallahs saved Nainital from further destructions. But, unfortunately, today there is no maintenance of these nallahs, though in the recent past some attempts have been made due to PIL of Prof. Ajay S. Rawat in Hon'ble High Court of Uttarakhand.

The Kailakhan Landslide and Ballia Ravine occurred in 1898 Nainital had to face the anger of nature again in the form of Ballia Ravine landslide. The Ballia Ravine, which is located at the lower end of the Nainital Lake, is important from the viewpoint that the overflow of the lake water passes through it. On the afternoon of 17 August 1898, a large chunk of the Kailakhan ridge slid down the Ballia Ravine. It temporarily filled some area of the Ballia Ravine; the area known as Brewery and some buildings below the ravine were submerged and caused the death of 27 Indians and one European. The cause of this landslide was deforestation and heavy rain, owing to which there was percolation of water into the surface layer. From August 9 to 17, 1898, Nainital experienced 91 cm of rainfall. After the catastrophe, stone walls and drains were constructed in the Ballia Nallah and Ballia Ravine, to prevent future landslides.

Furthermore, trees were planted on the bare land and unstable areas, and the management of forests in Nainital was laid down on the following lines:

1. To protect the hill sides from erosion.
2. To improve the quality and density of the plantations
3. To improve the scenery of the town by planting more trees.
4. To secure the maximum production of firewood and to ensure a sustained yield as far as possible

With the growth of Nainital, tourism and sale & purchase of land became a profitable business. Mary Jane Corbett, the mother of the famous Jim Corbett, took the initiative to promote tourism and rent out properties for the visitors who visited Nainital during the summers. The Hotel industry also got a boost in the years between 1870 and 1872 one of the finest hotels on the Mall Road was constructed. It was known as Mayo Hotel; later its name was changed to Albion Hotel and it got its present name as Grand Hotel in 1898. Gradually Nainital also became an important centre of trade and banking. In the 1880s the Bank of Upper India was established. Later in 1916 it was known as the Alliance Bank of Shimla and in 1923 as the Imperial Bank of India. In 1955 it was renamed as the State Bank of India. After establishment of the Bank of Upper India, the Allahabad Bank was established in 1892. Nainital soon became a centre of attraction for sports lovers and with their enthusiastic response the Nainital Gymkhana Club was formed in the year 1883 by the British. Tournaments and other competitive matches were started with hockey in the year 1890 and football in 1899. The same year cricket was also started with the formation of the Colvin Cricket Club under the patronage of His Highness the Maharaja of Balrampur. Besides other games, polo was also popular among the British. Polo matches, three a side, were played every alternate day on the flats, with two tournaments thrown in. The first was held in June to mark the Ranikhet week wherein the army teams from Ranikhet, Bareilly and Lucknow participated. The other was arranged in autumn as the I.C.S. week between the Eastern Command, the I.C.S. and the A.D.C. teams. Polo is a forgotten sight now. In 1935 it was discontinued owing to certain fatal accidents.

For conducting various tournaments, the Gymkhana officials used to erect a shamiyana in the initial stages. Later in 1903, Major Douglas Hunter, Honorary Secretary, Nainital Gymkhana applied for the lease of the open space near the Police Station, then used for erecting tents and *shamiyanas* during Ranikhet and Autumn weeks. The space was to be used for the construction of a wooden pavilion for cricket and polo players. By 1905 the old Pavilion had been constructed and was later replaced by the old Cricket Pavilion in 1925.

After the discontinuation of polo in 1935, the Gymkhana Committee constituted itself into the Nainital Gymkhana and the District Sports Association in 1936. Subsequently it was affiliated with the U.P. Sports Control Board. A move had been made in 1949 to raise funds for the renovation of the Cricket Pavilion, but it was only after 1956 that concerted efforts were made by the Government and the Municipal Board for the erection of a Sports Stadium in Nainital. In May 1959 the foundation stone was laid by late Dr. Rajendra Prasad, President of India and the Stadium was completed in 1963-64.

The flats have rightly been described as the activity centre of Nainital and are buzzing with activity almost throughout the year. Situated between the receding curves of hills and the charming background of the lake, it turns into a natural amphitheatre where numerous tournaments of different games are organized.

Sailing was introduced in Nainital in the year 1880 and the Nainital Sailing Club was formed in 1897. The earliest record of sailing on the Nainital Lake was in 1880, when the yachts sailed were of the cutter type with lead keels. This was the first time when Fleetwood Williams, I.C.S. Commissioner of Meerut, built a Schooner yacht at St. Asaphs and launched it on the lake by means of a trolley. A twin hulled boat, "Gemini' was also built and sailed by Colonel Henry, whilst Messrs Murray and Company imported three Belfast Lough type sailing boats, called 'Coya', 'Doodles' and 'Dorothy' and let them out on hire for several years.

The Nainital Sailing Club was started in 1897. The type of vessel used was the Skimming Dish or 'Sorceress' Type.

The well-known 'Wave' (Dee built) was of this class, and held her own for many years. Several yachts such as 'Spray' and 'Sheila' were locally built to compete with her, without much success.

In 1910, the Nainital Yacht Club was formed on the initiative of the Carey brothers C.W. Carey, a Major in the Guides, and F. Carey, a Captain in the Royal Artillery. Its name was entered in the Lloyds Register of Yachts in 1911. Those days, the Nainital Yacht Club had a fleet of nine yachts designed by Linton Hope and built by Turks and Co. of Kingston-on-Thames. It was affiliated to the Yacht Racing Association and had a membership of some 250 who were scattered all over India. The entrance fee was Rs. 30 with a monthly subscription of Rs. 10 per member. For temporary members, the fee was Rs. 15. The first Commodore of the Club was Sir W. Malcolm Hailey, G.C.I.E., K.C.S.I., I.C.S. and the Vice Commodore was Lt. Col. C.W. Carey. In 1948 the Club was taken over by the Indians and that year the Commodore was Sir Francis Verner Wyle and the Vice Commodore was Col. C.W. Carey. In 1951 for the first time an Indian, Raja Hari Chand Raj Singh was appointed the Rear Commodore of the Club and in 1957, Raj Kumar Giri Raj Singh was appointed as the first Indian Commodore of the Club. Rajkumar is credited with the promotion of yachting in Nainital.

It is interesting to note that the Nainital Yacht Club is the third oldest Sailing Club in India and perhaps the highest in the world. It has also the distinction of sailing the class of boats which are sailed nowhere else. The visitors even from abroad praise yachting and other facilities given to them by the Club today.

Theatre, both British and Hindi was also initiated during the period. Nainital was famous for the British Theatre and was accorded the same place as Shimla in the first decade of the 20 century. J.M. Clay, the author of the book, 'Nainital : A Historical and Descriptive Account' which was published in 1928 has written that, the drama has many houses in the Himalayas. If Shimla is the greatest, Nainital likes to believe itself not much behind". The only stage available in Nainital till 1921 was the one in the Assembly Rooms, the site of the present Capitol Cinema. The stage was too small and too deep for its breadth. The lighting consisted of oil lamps and the auditorium was badly shaped. Yet, on that stage, were produced such plays as "The Wilderness" (1910) a Drury Lane Melodrama, "The Three Little Maids" (1911), a musical comedy of the Gaiety type, "The Arccadians" (1913), which required the introduction of an aeroplane and a race horse; and "Iolanthe" (1916), with the outside of Westminister Hall for one of its scenes.

In 1921, the Club carried out a project which its committee had long been considering, and built a stage on to the Chalet ball-room. Here the facilities were much better. The Chalet as it is now known has a large stage, well lighted and well sloped.

One curious feature of Nainital theatre those days was the absence of any dramatic society. Untill 1912; the Nainital public depended for their plays entirely on the enterprise of individuals. In 1912, an Amateur Dramatic Society was formed, but its life, though merry, was short, for it died of debt in 1913. During the First World War, a committee was formed, known as the Nainital War Entertainment Committee, which, amongst other activities produced many good plays, the proceeds of which went to war charities. In 1923 this committee was renamed as the Amateur Dramatic Society.

Nainital was famous for its musical plays. In early days, these usually took the form of a burlesque, full of topical allusions, while the music was generally that of the popular airs of the day. Since 1922, there was a regular succession of the Gilbert and Sullivan operas, "Isolanthe", in 1922; "Patience", in 1923; "The Yeomen of the Guard", in 1924; "The Mikado", in 1925; "The Pirated of Penzance", in 1926; and in 1927, "the Gondoliers".

The European institutions were also centres of English plays. As late as 1956 "The Gondoliers" was staged by St. Joseph's College. In the 1950s the Shakespearian Dramatic Company used to come regularly to St. Joseph's and plays like "Henry the V", "Hamlet" and :The Merchant of Venice" were staged by their artistes. Even today popular and classical English plays are staged by these English medium institutions though in the town Hindi plays or translations of classical western plays are more popular.

The Bengalis introduced theatre in Nainital. The reason which can be attributed to this is the fact that those days when Nainital became the summer capital of the North Western Provinces, the majority of the clerks in the Secretariat were Bengalis. They are, by nature, art loving and to quench their thirst for theatre, they formed the Bengali Amateur Dramatic Club in 1884. The local inhabitants were inspired by them and they formed the Indian club in 1900 and the Friends Amateur Dramatic Club in 1910. During that early period, the plays staged were mostly epics like 'Arjun', 'Abhimanyu' and the 'Mahabharat' itself.

The Harihar Party also came into existence during that period and the Jan Sewak Sabha was formed in the year 1920-21. It was later named as the Union Dramatic Club. Concomitantly another dramatic club known as the Yuvak Mandali was established in Tallital.

The place of Friends Amateur Dramatic Club was taken up by the New Friend's Amateur Club in the year 1922-23.

The plays of the period were influenced by the Parsi Theatre and the plays staged were mostly of playwrights like Agha Hashr Kashmiri, Betab, Zeba and Radhey Shyam.

Then came the era of the walkie-talkie cinema which changed the taste of the audience in Nainital from theatre to movies. But the dramatist struggled to keep the spirit of theatre alive in Nainital and the credit for this struggle from 1933 to 1937 goes to the Happy Club. From 1938 to 1948 the Sharda Sangh shouldered the responsibility of reviving theatre in Nainital.

Sharda Sangh was originally called the Bhikka Club after its first president Mr. Bansi Lal Bhikka, established the Bhikka Orchestra which performed ballets and composed music. In 1943 the Club's name was changed to Sharda Sangh. It played an important role in the fifth and sixth decades of the last century in popularizing theatre. An added advantage for it was that the Chalet Hall in Nainital became available to Indian artistes with the dawn of independence in 1947.

A drama competition was held by Sharda Sangh for the first time in 1951 during the autumn festival under the aegis of the Nainital Municipality. All the plays in it were one act plays and six drama troupes participated. The competition was a great success and the first place went to the production "Chaurahey ke Atma' staged by the United Artistes Almora. The music was composed by Mr. Mohan Upreti and the play was directed by Mr. Brijendra Lal Sah. Both these artistes later achieved international repute. From 1952 to 1962 drama competitions were held annually in the Chalet Hall during the Autumn Festival and soon it became a nationally known drama competition. During this period many local artistes participated in competitions held at Lucknow, Delhi, Allahabad and Gwalior and achieved laurels for Nainital. Besides Sharda Sangh, many other clubs like the Naini Artistes Club came into existence but the credit of enthusing the spirit of theatre in Nainital goes to Sharda Sangh. An artist from Sharda Sangh, Late Mr. Brij Mohan Shah became Director of the National School of Drama, New Delhi and was internationally known.

A rapid growth took place in the late 19th century. In 1891, Nainital was declared a separate district, which also accelerated the development activities of the town as the district headquarters. Together with administrative units, government departments, several bungalows, rest houses, marketing areas, growth of recreational facilities like the clubs, dancing hall and theatres could be seen in Nainital. An important public building is Ramsay Hospital which was erected in 1892 in the memory of Sir Henry Ramsay, Commissioner of Kumaun (1856 to 1884), and later renamed as G.B. Pant Hospital. Another important building is the Crosthwaite Hospital (now known as B.D. Pande Hospital after the famous freedom fighter of Uttarakhand). It was established in 1896 by Sir Antony MacDowell on his first visit to Nainital as Lieutenant Governor. It was named after Sir Charles Crosthwaite, the preceding Lieutenant Governor. Cost of construction was, to a large extent, met by private contributions and a donation from Ramsay Hospital. The Crosthwaite Hospital was founded for Indian patients, whereas the Ramsay Hospital was for European patients. In the beginning it was intended for both, European and Indian patients, but this arrangement was found impracticable.

In 1899, the town was equipped with drinking water facilities since water works were established at Mallital. The population in February 1881 was 576, and inclusive of the visitors it was 10,054 in September 1880. By 1891, the population was increased by 8455. These figures show that by 1880 the town had already emerged as a popular summer resort and educational centre.

URBANISATION THROUGH EUROPEAN SCHOOLS

The European schools for boys and girls were considered separately, as they bore no special relation to the education of the district, but are rather provincial in character, pupils coming to them from all parts of the United Provinces and elsewhere. The European boys' schools in Nainital were opened as high schools. These include the Diocesan Boys' School, St. Joseph's Seminary, a Roman Catholic institution which also is knowns as a College, the Oak Openings School on Sher-ka-Danda belonging to the American Mission, the Priory and the Hermitage. The girls' schools comprise the All Saints' Diocesan High School, the Wellesley high school, also owned by the American Missionaries, St. Mary's Convent, and Miss Parkinson's School as Porterfield was also opened. The Nainital Diocesan Schools owe their origin to a project formed by Dr. Condon, Mr. H.S. Roid and others in 1800; for founding a school for the children of residents and others of small means. In July 1800 a mixed school was commenced and continued during the next year, with such success that the committee decided upon enlarging the scheme and setting up two schools, one for boys and the other for girls. These schools were commenced on the 1st of February, 1871, and have met in the house known as Rohilla Lodge, but in 1878 Sherwood, which has been used by Sir Henry Ramsay as residence and bought from him by General Huthwaite of the Bengal Artillery, was purchased by the committee and continued to be used as a school till 1896, when it was bought as a residence for the Lieutenant Governor. The school was then located temporarily in a building on the site of the present Secretariat. The present school building on the south-east side of Ayarpatha was started in 1896 and completed two years later.

The aided secondary schools in the district comprise the Secondary Diamond Jubilee high school and the American Mission School at Nainital. The latter was founded in 1858, and has lastly been raised to the status of a high school.

The Mission School, where the present C.R.S.T. Intermediate College is housed, is the oldest educational institution in Nainital and was established in1850. In 1908 it was taken over as Humphrey High School and in 1928 it became a Vernacular school owing to the efforts of Lala Chetram Sah Thulgharia. The same year it was named as C.R.S.T. Intermediate College. Humphrey High School where the present CRST Intermediate College is housed was the first educational institution in Nainital.

Sherwood College is supposed to be the oldest European School in Nainital. It was established in July 1867 and grew out of the need for a good school in a healthy climate for the education of European boys of modest means. Today Sherwood is considered as one of the premier institutions in India. The Diocesan Boys' School was founded by Bishop Milman of Calcutta. The original site was at Stoneleigh, where now the Ramsay Hospital stands. In 1873, the school was transferred to Sherwood.

The next school which came into existence was **All Saints College,** which is one of the best girls' institutions in the country today. It caters to the all round development of its students. The All Saints' Diocesan Girls' School was founded at the same time as the Diocesan Boys' School, and the two constituted one establishment. When, however, the boys moved to Sherwood, a separation took place, and the girls went to Peter's field until 1874, when they moved to Barns dale. In November 1869 it was formally established with only two students. Miss Bradbury was appointed as the teacher. The main objective was to educate European girls of modest income and with the vicissitudes of changing times; the school has made no compromise in maintaining high standards of education.

The first Catholic institution, **St. Mary's Convent** was founded in 1878 by the Reverend to Mother Salesia Reiner, the Superiors of the Institute of the Blessed Virgin Mary. The school started in 1878 in a rented house, Belvedere, which is now owned by the Raja Sahib of Awagarh State Raja Aniruddha Singh. During the formative weeks, Mother Salesia realized the necessity of buying an estate where a convent and school could be built. Eventually her search led her to Ramsay Park, the property of Sir Henry Ramsay, the Commissioner of Kumaun. She recognized the place as the one she had seen in a dream as a child and immediately requested an interview with Sir Henry Ramsay to conclude negotiations for its purchase. St. It is now situated at Ramnee Park.

On 4th January, 1879 the sisters moved in the newly acquired estate. Subsequently, a chapel was established, but it soon proved too small, and on 2nd February, 1880 the foundation stone of the present church was laid.

The estate is now known as Ramnee Park and the school is also locally known as Ramnee School. The name Ramnee is an aberration of Ramsay; as the servants working in the estate, were unable to pronounce the name correctly, addressed Sir Ramsay as 'Ramnee Sahib'. Eleven years after the sisters arrived in Nainital, on 12th of May, 1889, the vision was realized and the school was solemnly blessed by the bishop of Allahabad.

St. Joseph's College is another Catholic institution, which was also born in the nineteenth century. Originally the St. Joseph's Seminary of Darjeeling was housed here;

hence the popular name Sem of St. Joseph's College. In 1887 that district was transferred by the ecclesiastical authorities in Rome to the Archbishop in Calcutta. St. Joseph's College is a school for the Roman Catholic diocese of Allahabad. An account of its arrival in 1888 from Darjeeling has already been given. Rev. Dr. Pesci was Bishop of Allahabad those days, and with the sundering of Darjeeling from his diocese, the question of a site for a good school for the sons of his Catholic flock became pressing. The building of St. Joseph's College was completed in 1888, and was opened by Sir Auckland Colvin, Lieutenant-Governor. The arrival of St. Joseph's College in Nainital was due to the transfer in 1887 by the authorities in Rome of Darjeeling from the diocese of Allahabad to tilted archdiocese of Calcutta. Hitherto, the school for Catholics of the Allahabad Diocese had been at Darjeeling, where Father Eaglebert, O.N.C. presided over St. Joseph's Seminary. It was now moved to Nainital, still under Father Eaglcbert. The pupils arrived towards the end of January 1888, and, until their new premises were ready, lived in a rented house, Long View, a few yards away from the College. The site was purchased from a Mr. Read for Rs. 72,000, and the building cost Rs. 47,000. The large playing field was subsequently purchased at a cost of Rs. 500 per acre.

Father Englebert and his pupils entered the new building on March 1st, 1889. On April, 22 1892, the Seminary passed under its present management to the Irish Christian brothers in Calcutta. Pending this change from the Seminary to the school, Father Englebert went to Ranikhet as the Military Chaplain.

In 1905 the **Philander Smith College** came into existence. Philander Smith College is the result of the amalgamation of the Oak Openings Boys' High School. The latter was founded by a Mrs. Smith, widow of Mr. Philander Smith of Illinois. Her interest in the education of the Anglo-Indian and domiciled European community had been awakened through the influence of the Reverend Davis Osborne of the Methodist Episcopal Church, who opened the school in 1885. Oak Openings School was opened by the Reverend J .W. Waugh, D.D., of the Methodist Episcopal Church, in 1880 at Stoneleigh, which, since its evacuation by the Diocesan Boys' School, had been occupied by the Lieutenant-Governor. It moved to its present site in 1889. In 1905, took place the union with the school at Mussoorie, which had outgrown till accommodation there. The site of the school in Murlinagar Estate on the road above Landour Bazar in Mussorie was restricted and therefore it was decided that the school should be shifted to Nainital. In January 1905, the school was united with the Oak Opening High School, whose splendid site afforded ample room for expansion. The magnificent location is reputed to be the highest in India for an institution of this kind. It is 342 m above the lake and over 2136 m above the sea level. From 1942 to 1946 it was named as the Hallet War School, after the last governor of the United Provinces for specific purpose of accommodating the children of the war personnel. In 1946 the estate was acquired by Birla Vidya Mandir. The possession of the estate was obtained in April 1947 and Birla Vidya Mandir was formally opened on July 17th, 1947. Today it is one of the prestigious institutions of the country.

Another school, which was considered as a premier institution during the 19th century, was the **Wellesley's Girls High School.** At the annual conference of the Methodist Episcopal Church of 1882, Miss E.K. Knowles was appointed to open a school for European girls in Nainital. As Miss Knowles was a graduate of Wellesley

College in United States, it was decided to name the girls' school after her alma mater. The school was first housed in buttress Castle below Ramsay Hospital. From Buttress Castel it was moved to South Wood and from there to Forest Lodge, as the number started increasing. In 1884 the school bought the beautifully situated Smuggler's Rock estate, half way to the top of Ayarpata hill. For three years the school was housed in the old building on the estate, then in 1887 it moved into the permanent home, the new stone building that was erected. At present DSB Campus of Kumaun University is located here.

RELIGIOUS SHRINES OF NAINITAL

Nainital was also a famous religious center during the early years of its settlement. Nainital has been famous place for the followers of Christianity owing to its scenic beauty and serenity. Nainital is also famous for its communal harmony. In the Flats area, the ground inn Mallital, one can see the Temple, Mosque, Gurudwara, the Arya Samaj and the Methodist Church located very close to each other. It is the oldest Methodist church of India and perhaps that of Asia.

TEMPLES

The *Naina Devi* temple already existed here before the advent of the British. It was then located near the present Boat House Club and was constructed by Lala Moti Ram Sah a contractor, who is credited to have constructed the earliest buildings of Nainital. After the landslide of 1880 one of the bells of the temple was excavated near the present site and the present temple was completed here in 1883.

The tradition of the temple of *Pashan Devi* is interwoven with G.W. Traill the Commissioner of Kumaun, who was equally popular as the legendary Sir henry Ramsay. The temple is sited on the *Thandi Sarak* towards Tallital and the

Goddess *Nav Durga* is worshipped here. She is a form of *Shakti* and a manifestation of *Saraswati, Laxmi* and *Parvati*. Each of these three deities gives rise to three more forms and hence in all these nine forms she is known as *Nav Durga*. She is the Goddess of vitality and power.

Another important temple of the same period is *Gufa Mahado* or Lord Shiva's Cave temple in close proximity to the Krishnapur Estate. The estate is named after Rais Krishna Sah who constructed the temple after his wife saw Lord Shiva in a dream. She was a very pious persons and a great devotee of Lord Shiva. On the auspicious day of *Maha Shivaratri*, She clearly heard in her dream that Lord Shiva is beckoning her that he is underneath in cave. The cave was excavated and buried below a huge boulder, a beautiful stone in the shape of a phallus was found. When it was unearthed, it was emitting a strong light and exuded the transcendental glory of the almighty. For a brief spell everyone was blinded by the glare but soon they recovered and at the behest of Rais Krishna Sah a temple was constructed at the site in 1892. He financed the construction of the temple and soon it assumed importance as a centre for ascetics and a retreat for the devotees of Lord Shiva.

A temple though constructed in the recent past, on 16th June 1953, and deserves mention, is the *Hanuman Garhi* temple. It is at a distance of 3.22 km from town on the Haldwani road and has developed as a great religious centre. The temple is a highly charged place and was constructed by the famous saint *Neeb Karauri* who lived in the 20th Centruy. He appeared to be an ordinary human being, but was actually a divine incarnate. His actions revealed an all knowing, all pervading and all powerful being that had nature itself under his command. Baba ji is regarded as a symbol of hope in the quagmire of this illusionary life and the temple has become a new monastery of repose, where we all become on. People of different faiths and religions visit this divine retreat, which guides us to be in harmony with our inner self and our Gods.

Hanuman Garhi is very famous for its sunset views and for the surreal designs that the clouds weave during the rainy season. The temple is surrounded by a rich forest and is a haven for bird watching and also for wild life.

In close proximity to the temple is Aryabhatta Research Institute of Astronomical Studies (ARIES). It was established in Varanasi on April 20th, 1954 as the State Observatory of Uttar Pradesh. In November 1955, it was shifted to Nainital and housed in a small cottage, Devi Lodge and then to the present site in Manora Peak. ARIES, which also signifies the Zodiacal sign of sun has made significant contribution in several areas of astronomical research, particularly those involving time critical phenomenon. ARIES presently hosts five telescopes of sizes 15 cm, 38 cm, 52 cm, 56 cm and 104 cm.

Another temple recent origin, which is very popular, is the *Shiva* Temple in Snow View. Devotees from far flung places visit this holy place to discover the essence of truth and eternal life. About the temple it is well known that the unfulfilled wishes and aspirations of the people are fulfilled here in unseen tangible ways. From Snow View as the name suggests an indescribably beautiful and breath taking picture of the glittering Himalayas can be seen.

Then there is the famous *Sipahi Dhara* temple near Tallital, which symbolizes the sustainable use of natural resources. Water is a precious gift of nature and its use is as old as civilization itself. In Kumaun water is revered and regarded as sacred and before and during the British rule, the use of water was sanctified and the water bodies were well maintained unlike today. The lake of Nainital was propitiated as Goddess *Parvati*, the reincarnation of

Sati and nobody dared to defile the lake, but today it has become a dumping ground for many people. They are not realizing that it is the life line of the city and the main source of sustenance.

Dhara is a common source of drinking water and can be compared with a drinking water fountain. In Nainital there are still many dharas, though some of them have dried up owing to excessive construction and encroachment. The worship in the temple of *Sipahi dhara* is to remind us that water is an economic commodity with multiple uses and protection of fresh water resources and the lake is the need of the hour for water management, and it should be used judiciously.

Nainital is an amalgamation of various cultural groups of different castes. Religions and creeds with complete cohesiveness from which, it draws its prominent feature unity in diversity. Nature has therefore played an important role in shaping the concept of Gods and Goddesses and in Nainital there are two important temples of the local deities, Lord *Gangnath* and Lord *Golla* the God of Justice.

The temple *Gangnath* is very old though it was renovated in 1982. It is situated on the outskirts of the Himalayan Zoo in Nainital. *Gangnath* is the lord of the proletariat and his temples are found throughout Kumaun. The temple of *Gangnath* in Nainital is a treasure trove and an epitome of human faith and belief. He is propitiated here as a messenger of hope and a healer of human souls. Lord *Gangnath* is not only a local deity but a spiritual teacher to the seekers who come to this temple. According to tradition,*Gangnath* was born in a feudal family. He was the son of *Udeychand,* the lord of the principality of Doti in Nepal. He had a solar lineage. When *Gangnath* was born, his father requested the court astrologer to prepare his son's horoscope and also to foresee his future. The astrologer forecasted that the boy was blessed with all virtues except by the time he will attain the age of twelve, he would renounce the world. At the predicted age it was also believed that he would marry *Bhana Bamini, a Brahmin* girl and subsequently renounce the world. To prove the forecast wrong, *Udeychand* decided that he would tie the nuptial knot of his son with a princess of his choice and then change her name to *Bhana Bamini*. Later, on the advice of his courtiers, he married his son seven times before he reached the age of twelve with iron statues. But destiny could not be changed and at the age of twelve, *Gangnath* actually fell in love with *Bhaana*. She hailed from a Joshi family and was a resident of the village *Daniya Kurkauli* near Almora. It is said that *Gangnath* saw her for the first time in a dream. Later he went to the village on a horse back and donned the garb of a mendicant so tht he could not be recognized. When he arrived at the village, *Bhana* saw him from the window. It is stated that she was awaiting him and immediately hauled him to her room with a rope. After this incident he used to meet her regularly. The Joshi clan did not approve of this clandestine relationship and in consequence of a wicked intrigue murdered him. He then became a ghost and the Joshi's to appease him built a temple of *Gangnath* and started worshipping him.

Although the stronghold of the Brahmanical Gods and Goddesses has remained stronger, more dominating, the local deities have also attained sufficient importance. The temples of *Gangnath* have been established throughout Kumaun as he is identified with the proletariat. Among the peasantry in distress they resort to Lord *Gangnath* and also invoke him. Basically Lord *Gangnath* is a manifestation of class struggle and he undoes the injustice inflicted upon the oppressed classes.

The temple of *Golu Devta* or Lord *Golla* is located on

the *Thandi Sarak* and was recently build. Lord *Golla* is venerated by the people as the God of Justice and as a source of light amidst the dark clouds of injustice inflicted upon the poor and the oppressed.

He is worshipped by the masses as an epitome of justice and is the most propitiated folk god of Kumaun. *Golu Devta,* according to the popular folk lore, was a scion of the Rai dynasty of the principality of *Dhumakot* under the Chand Kings. The progenitor of this dynasty was *Jhalarai* who came to power during the 15th century A.D. his fief was surrounded by thick forests and his subjects depended more on forest produce than agricultural pursuits. The feudal lords also sustained on forest produce and perambulated through forests in search of food and game.

Jhalarai's successor, his son, *Halarai* was famous for his intrepidity and hunting skills. The next in line, *Golla* was born from the eighth wife of *Halarai* and was his only male progeny. It is said that after marrying seven wives when he could not father a son, *Halarai* became very sad and requested the court astrologer to predict his future. The astrologer told him that a son would be born to him from his eighth spouse. One day *Halarai* went to the forest for hunting and after roaming in the woods on horseback for several hours, he became very thirsty. To quench his thirst he went to a nearby hut where a beautiful damsel *Kalika* met him. He was attracted by her magnetic charm and requested her to marry him. She agreed and soon the nuptial ceremony was solemnized. Subsequently they returned to *Halarai's* fief and lived happily. But the seven wives were very envious of Kalka's beauty. They despised her and left no opportunity to humiliate and conspire against her. With the vicissitudes of time the feeling of jealousy aggravated; they were looking for a chance to harm her and soon they got an opportunity. *Halarai* went out for hunting one day and in his absence *Kalika* was blessed with a son. The seven wives hatched a conspiracy. They tied a cloth around the mother's eye during the child birth on the pretext of warding off the evil eye and later told her that she had given birth to a *sil batta,* a grinding stone. The newly born child was then put in a small wooden box and thrown into the river Gori. Fortunately a fisherman found the box while fishing. The fisherman opened the box and was delighted to see the child. According to tradition as the child was retrieved from the river Gori, he was named as *Goriya*. With the passage *Goriya* became *Gorlla* and later *Golla*. When *Halarai* returned home, he was told about the incident that *Kalika* had given birth to a *sil batta*. He was so infuriated that he abandoned her.

When *Golla* came of age, the treachery was revealed to him by his adoptive father. *Golla* took a vow to avenge the injustice meted out to his mother and was looking for an opportune moment. It is said that one day he took a wooden horse to a spring where the seven wives of *Halarai* had come with their entourage. He then put the horse's mouth into the spring and started coaxing it to drink water. On witnessing the sight, the seven women started to laugh and commented, "Hey crazy man, how can wooden horse drink water." *Golla* retorted that if a woman can give birth to a *sil batta,* then a wooden horse can also drink water. The news of the incident spread like a forest fire and *Halarai* also came to know about it. He was then convinced that his seven wives had conspired against him. He took immediate action against them and *Golla* was then made the lord of the fief. His mother's prestige was also restored and she was called back to the palace.

Dhumagarh was one of the principalities of Kumaun which was being ruled by the Chand dynasty. *Golla* was later elevated to the position of the general of the Chand army owing to his integrity and popularity. He was a brave warrior and had led the Kumauni army to several victories. He was also an ace horse rider and his mount was a white steed. It is believed that in one of the battles, probably against the Nepalese he was killed in action. Since he had laid his life for his people, he was elevated to the status of a demi god and the Kumauni's started worshipping him.

Today he is regarded as a symbol of gallantry by the people of Kumaun and also a God of Justice. His lore of bravery and justice are sung by the local artists in different fairs and festivals. People, who have been subjected to humiliation and injustice, go to his temple and plead their cases. The appellants can petition on a plain or on stamp paper and people strongly believe that he showers his divine justice with a strong hand.

CHURCHES

One of the earliest buildings erected in Nainital was the church, St. Johns in the Wilderness. The site was chosen as early as 1844; the corner stone was laid down in October 1846 and was first opened on April 2nd 1848. In 1856, it was taken over as a public building by the Government. The legendary hunter, conservationist and writer Jim Corbett was baptized here.

THE FIRST METHODIST CHURCH OF INDIA

The construction of the church was started in 1858 and dedicated to the people on October 1860. It was established by an American Methodist Missionary, William Butler with the help of Sir Henry Ramsay. William Butler who belonged to the Methodist Episcopal Church in Areria,Bihar came to Calcutta on September 22nd 1856. When he stepped on the Indian soil the political climate was not congenial for missionary work. After visiting several places in India with his family he settled down in Bareilly in 1857. He had scarcely begun work when on May 10th 1857; three regiments in Meerut revolted and the repercussion of the conflagration were felt in Bareilly also. On 14th may the Commanding Officer of Bareilly advised him to go to Nainital, which was a safe refuge for the British refugees. The journey to Nainital was accomplished without any incident. After the outbreak of 1857 was over, Butler purchased land for the church and the parsonage. The church is now a heritage site and every year thousands of devotees and tourists visit the holy place to listen to the deepest wisdom of their soul. A visit to the church is an exhilarating experience because the mind in this blissful place does not deliberate between the domain of the past events or apprehensions of the future. The moments spent here belong to the present and are devoid of the constant struggle that ensues in the mind of what is and what ought to be. In 1868 another Methodist Church was established near the present Tallital bus station by Rev. William Butler to cater to the religious needs of the bourgeoning congregation. In 1971 this church was converted to Bishop Shaw School by Rev. Bishop A.J. a great educationist. Today it is the best English medium institution in and around Nainital for students from a humble background.

ST. NICHOLAS CHURCH

Close to the entry point of Raj Bhawan is one of the most beautiful Protestant churches of the town, St. Nicholas Church, whose foundation stone was laid in 1890 and consecrated in 1896 by Rev. Bishop Alfred Clifford and Sir Auckland Colvin, the lt. Governor of the North Western province and the Commissioner of Oudh. The structure of the church is very imposing and here light seems to triumph over substance. It projects the universe in microcosm and is a home of peace and praise to God.

CATHOLIC CHURCH

Another important church of the period is the St. Francis Catholic Church towards the lower side of the lake. It is popularly known as the Lake Church and was built as a chapel in 1868 by Father Macen of the Vicarate of Agra. It was dedicated to St. Francis of Assisi. Concomitantly the St. Francis Hoke was established din 1895 by father Petronius Granunga.

Later on the Lake Chapel proved small for the increasing congregation and hence rebuilding of the present church began in 1907 and blessed on 23rd May 1909 by the Archbishop of Agra, Rev. Charles Gentili. Now it belongs to the Diocese of Bareilly. The charm of this church is its simplicity and the ambience of the quiet engenders here to look within and make you understand that the mundane processions make life more complicated and we do not know even and where to stop.

MOSQUE

The mosque was constructed in 1865 originally built for Muslim soldiers in the British army. The symmetrical emphasis associated with Islamic architecture, the lush decoration, and the minarets from which the callof the prayer is sounded. The most notable feature is the Mihrab where a niche shows the direction towards Mecca it was renovated in the year 2004-2005

GURUDWARA

The first Gurudwara came into existence in Nainital around 1897. During the period when Raj Bhawan was under construction, the Ramgarhia Sikhs from Punjab were especially invited for masonry work owing to their excellent craftsmanship. They built the first Gurudwara in the Raj Bhawan premises. Later in 1923, five Sikhs who were posted here in the Eastern Command realized the Gurudwara is located in thick forest with wild animals and owing to its location was difficult to visit for worship. They decided to shift it from the wilderness to a suitable locality in the town. Thereafter, the same year it was established in Jai Bhawan in the middle of Tallital bazaar. In 1935 the location was again changed and the Gurudwara was shifted to Mallital bazar in 1935 and in May 1947 it was finally transferred to its present site where the foundation stone was laid by the eminent Sikh leader, Master Tara Singh.

ARYA SAMAJ MANDIR

The Arya Samaj was initiated as the Satya Dharma Prakashni Sabha in Nainital. Influenced by the philosophy of Maharshi Dayanand Saraswati, Pandit Gajanand Chimwal and his associates established this Sabha on 20th May 1874. This was the beginning of the Arya SamajMovement in Nainital. On Wednesday 7th April 1875 when Maharshi Dayanand Saraswati established the Arya Samaj in Bombay, the members of the Satya Dharma Prakashmi Sabha joined hands with the Arya Samaj. The present site of Arya Samaj Mandir was allotted to it after independence owing to the effort of Mr. Jasod Singh Bisht, the then Chairman of the Municipal Board, Nainital and Mr. R.B. Shivdasani, the then Commissioner of Kumaun.

EARLY TWENTIETH CENTURY URBAN DEVELOPMENT (1900-1947)

Manypublic utility services were started during the period but the development process in town was reported a bit slow in early decades of twentieth century. Government House was constructed down the slope of Sher-ka-Danda, but was declared unsafe because of the historical landslide of 1880, and hence, a new, most beautiful building the 'Government House' was built in the south western section of the town near Sherwood estate in 1900. The magnificent Raj Bhawan is the most gorgeous building of the colonial period. The foundation stone was laid on April 27, 1897 and was completed in March 1900. The Raj Bhawan stands upon a plateau with rising ground behind it, which screens it from a precipitous cliff ridge, and a sunken lawn fringed with deodar trees. The combined effect of its environs, the vividly green lawn, grey stone steps and a well grown forest is dignified, peaceful and strongly reminiscent of the English country side. From the level of the lower lawn, a well graded path traverses the outlying portion of the grounds where the 18 holes old golf course lies, which is one of the best golf courses in Northern India. For draining out the water from the golf course, an underground tunnel, 137.1 meters in length has been constructed in the lowest bowl of the course, a marvel of engineering skill. The area of Raj Bhawan is 82 ha. consist of hill and forest. It has been designed after the Buckingham palace and the architecture has been professionally described of the early Gothic style. The material is grey stone though some Agra red stone has been used for its ornamentation of the facade and railings. The front aspect is dominated by the six castellated turrets, which in the beginning were crowned by steep pinnacles. The general effect of the building is one of solidity and dignity without exuberance. The back view of the house, which also nearly suggests an English country house, is, perhaps its most beautiful aspect. The Raj Bhawan has a rich collection of the 19 and 20 centuries' weapons like lances, swords, muzzle loaders etc. including the weapons of the legendary bandit Sultana Daku, elephant tusks and other trophies and collection of medals and antique furniture.

A grand secretariat building now known as Uttarakhand High Court was also constructed in 1900. In this period many public utility services were also commenced in the town. An important building of that period is the Tallital Post Office, which was constructed according to the records of the Postal Department in 1896. The Mallital Post Office however came into existence in 1903. This building was constructed as per geographical conditions of the town and constructed from light weight material. There is another attractive building of YWCA (Young Women Christian Association) now the Hotel Fair Havens is situated in the building. In 1910 a telephone exchange was established in Mallitals and a local hydel power station was established downstream Balia Nallah at Durgapur in 1922. The construction of rail link to Kathgodam in 1884 and the completion of a motorable road between Kathgodam and Nainital in 1915 were significant factors that helped in the early growth of the town. Owing to these facilities Nainital attracted spur in tourism activities. Within the town, development of a network of bridle paths connected several areas, again gave a momentum to the process of urbanization.

There was absence of good theatre experienced in Nainital until 1921. In 1921 the British carried out a project and built a stage in the Chalet Ball Room, which is now famous as Chalet Hall. With the dawn of Independence, Chalet Hall became available to Indians. Nainital achieved recognition for Hindi Journalism and is credited for starting the publication of the first Hindi newspaper, Samay Vinod in Uttarakhand in 1868. Most of the editorials of this paper focused on the socio-economic conditions of the local people and of the repressive policies of the British. Concomitantly some important buildings like the Collectorate and the Police Lines was constructed.

Since 1841 to 1900 there were only 40 major bungalows in Nainital town, but by 1927, 326 houses near civil line area, 290 in Mallital bazaar and 279 in Tallital bazaar were built, which reached up to 2839 by the year 1939. There was sluggishness in the growth and development of Nainital during the period 1931-1947 due to the world wars and the freedom struggle.

During this period Nainital became the Eastern Command Army Headquarters and Summer Capital of Northwest Province. After it was made the summer capital, a remarkable expansion of the town occurred with the growth of magnificent bungalows, construction of facilities such as marketing areas, rest houses, recreation centers, clubs, etc. together with the secretariat and other administrative units. It also became an important centre of education for the British. The 36 km long Kathgodam – Nainital road was completed during the time and electric supply was available to the town. Almost 925 buildings were constructed up till 1900.

Another important building of the early 20 century was Gurney House where Jim Corbett the legendary conservationist started residing since 1919. He returned to Nainital finally in 1919 after spending 21 years in Mokameh Ghat, where he worked as trans-shipment inspector in the railways and also handled the contract for trans-shipment of merchandise. After returning to Nainital, he took active interest in city politics and was appointed as a member of the Nainital Municipal Board on 2 April 1919. In 1923 he became the Senior Vice-Chairman of the Municipal Board. He was passionately in love with Nainital. After becoming the member of

Nainital Municipal Board he donated Rs. 7300 to the board for the benefit of the town. Out of this amount a band stand on the shore of the lake was constructed and land for the cremation ghat, near Pines below Bhowali road was acquired. As Nainital was very rich in bird life he wanted to declare Nainital into a bird sanctuary but did not succeed. Even today Nainital and the surrounding areas are a haven for bird watchers. He took an extra interest in protecting the town's natural surroundings and at his instance bye laws were framed in 1937 for licensing for goats as they did a lot of damage in the Municipal forests. Again owing to his efforts fishing was not permitted in Nainital Lake during night time and use of artificial lights for fishing was banned.

In this way the town gradually developed and the trends of growth of the town are more or less reflected in the growth of population in the town. The Census of 1901 recorded a population of 7609. The marginal fall in population during the decade 1921 to 1931 might have been due to the great recession of late twenties and the thirties. This might have adversely affected both the stakeholders, predominated by the tertiary sector and the population. The decline in the population of the town during the decade 1931-1941 can be attributed of the decision of the first provincial Congress Government of 1937 not to move the Summer Capital of Nainital and the impact of the Second World War. This resulted in a large fall in the number of persons visiting Nainital. The shifting of the army headquarters of the Eastern Command from Nainital to Ranchi could have also affected the population of the town. After independence, Nainital continued to function as UP Government's summer capital. The towns' growing popularity as tourist centre spurted construction of numerous hotels along Mall Road and Sher-ka-Danda area. The population increased between 1941 and 1951 can be attributed partly to the regained status as the summer capital of the state after independence. The end of the Second World War, and the changes ushered in the new opportunities brought by independence were also responsible for growth of the population of this hill resort.

Although Nainital had achieved sufficient fame as a hill resort due to its scenic beauty and attraction of the lake before 1947, the town still remained as headquarters to different government offices and a hill resort to high-class gentry. Thus, only a compact class of the society enjoyed the township of Nainital before 1947. It was only after Independence that the town started its expansion and a concentration of population, largely engaged in secondary and tertiary activities, began in the town.

The post-Independence period has been associated with many fundamental and interesting changes in the growth of the town. While many of the changes are associated with corresponding changes in the International tourist map, some of the changes have been local in nature or peculiar to Nainital.

CHAPTER-4

Urbanization After Independence

DEVELOPMENT AFTER INDEPENDENCE (1947-1960)

The decade following Independence was a period of slow growth with shifting of the major administrative functions and little recognition of the town as a tourist resort. It was also a lean period for tourism activities. For some time, senior bureaucrats, ministers and some officials moved to Nainital for only 6 to 8 weeks during the summers. The efforts of the U.P. Government to popularize tourism brought result in 1956, when the government established a separate Department of Tourism in the State. As a result of this, and also due to other factors, the tourist traffic of Nainital rose steadily during the latter part of the fifties.

PERIOD OF GRADUAL DEVELOPMENT (1961-1980)

This phase began with a great setback to the growth of the town when in 1960, the State Government decided not to shift the capital of Nainital in summers due to a number of factors. In the initial stages, this step proved to be a big blow to the tourist activity and the economy of the town. But, it soon started reviving its lost significance as a leading tourist resort. In 1960, the State Government had already established a Regional Tourist Bureau at Nainital with a view to promote tourism in the hill areas. This also helped to some extent in recovery and subsequent growth of tourism activity in the town. The Indo-Pak wars of 1965 and 1971 gave a boost of tourism in Nainital since a large number of tourists avoided visiting Kashmir during these years. The annual tourist inflow in the two main seasons during the years 1961 to 1965 was recorded as 92,387, 98,178, 91,335, 1, 08,060 and 1,36,986, respectively.

It is clear from the above data there was a big surge (27%) in the tourist activity in 1965 and the increasing requirements led to the growth of hotel and other such accommodations in the town. While there were only 15 hotels in 1951, their number rose to 20 in 1961 and to 30 in 1971. A number of new settlements were established and the number of households increased to more than 3742 in 1961, and 4053 in 1971 as compared to 2899 in 1950 and 2829 in 1941. The functions of the town also increased. Kumaun University, to which Government Degree Colleges and Higher Educational Institutions of Kumaun region are affiliated, was established in 1973, is the largest State University of Uttarakhand. To facilitate and encourage the tourist industry in the region of Kumaun, a development agency known as 'Kumaun Mandal Vikas Nigam' was established in 1976. The increasing number of tourists in the town encouraged commissioning of numerous travel agencies since 1980's around the region. In 1970, the construction of a new road between Nainital and Kaladhungi was started that was completed in 1975. The population data of 1951, 1961 and 1971 also shows a steady rise in the population, which was 13,093, 16,080 and 25,167 in the respective year. By 1972, the town had emerged as a full-fledged tourist town.

RECENT DEVELOPMENT: PERIOD OF RAPID GROWTH (1980-PRESENT DAY)

The third or the latest phase is related with the diversification of the functions of the town including its rising status such as an internationally famous hill resort. The increased tourist flow has not only had an impact on the economy of the town but has equally influenced its evolution and the functional morphology. The new functions emerged in the field of higher and other educations institutions and a variety of services that cater to the needs of the tourists such as hotels, restaurants, travel agencies, transport, holiday homes and tourists guide services. This phase may, therefore, be associated with a phenomenal increase in the built-up area of the town mainly in the shape of tourist facilities along the Mall Road, the main thoroughfare of the town. At the two ends of the lake are found congested markets with three to five storied houses. The surrounding ridges constitute the residential units, although such houses are also found near the Mall Road that goes along the lake.

During this period many new establishments were set-up, such as, the electronic telephone exchange in 1982, Television Relay Tower in 1984, High Altitude Zoo in 1984 and the ropeway in 1985. Modernization of the public facilities such as the sewer lines, drinking water supply was also undertaken. Under a statutory authority known as Greater Nainital Lake Development Authority, the U.P. Government had envisaged an ambitious development plan for a phased implementation in and around Nainital town – keeping in view the current needs of town expansion as also the most pressing problems of the day. With the creation of the new hill state of Uttarakhand, followed the decision to make Nainital the seat of its High Court a function which has not only increased the area of its influences, which now extends across the entire state of Uttarakhand. In consequence, a vast area surrounding the former Secretariat building has been converted into High Court Campus with several large and small buildings housing the High Court and associated offices together with many others, such as club and residential areas of the members of the judiciary. Most of the district offices have been shifted to the Vikas Bhawan at Bhimtal. Correspondingly, there has been a significant increase in the population of the town with development, and according to the census of the 1981, 1991 and 2001 the population was 26,093, 30,945 and 39,911, respectively. A number of new residences were established which increased to 5456 in 1981, 7850 in 1991 and 8358 settlements in 2001, 10537 in 2011 census. Conspicuously, the decadal growth rate of 43% in 1901 - 11 decade dropped to 10 % low in the following decade. Still more conspicuous, as the available data indicates, is that Nainital had negative growth rate in the decade 1921-31 (- 9%), and no growth at all (0%) in the following decade. These phenomena gives clear indication that during these two decades there had been a large exodus of population from this town. For, even the natural growth of population in the 1931 decade was overtaken by the rate of out-migration, and in the decade of 1941 was evened out by the rate of population exodus from the town. This situation was not repeated in the later decades but the trend of growth rate has not been smooth.

The decades 1961-71 and 1971-81 held some big surprises. While in the former decade the decadal growth rate shot up to as high as 71%, in the later decade it recorded a 4% low. By implication, 4% decadal growth rate (i.e. less than 0.5 % per annum) being much lower than even the natural growth rate of population in India, it may be inferred that in this decade also, Nainital was de-populated. In the decade 1981-91 the growth rate shot up to 20%, and in 1991-2001 decade it recorded 26.67%, exceeding the national average of 21.53% for the same decade. In 1880 habitat was restricted to 18% part of the town but today in 2011 it has been increased to 40%.

CHAPTER-5

Conclusion

PROBLEMS AND CONSTRAINS OF URBAN DEVELOPMENT IN NAINITAL

Nainital Lake Township is a prime example of Urbanisation which is severely impacted by the human activities. It has become a popular hill resort apart from its natural beauty, wilderness, lakes, climate, accessibility and a number of other opportunities and facilities that are seldom found in such an appropriate combination in any other hill station in the country. The increased tourist influx has a significant impact on the economy of the town. It has also a great impact in increasing the functions and services pertaining to tourism and it is because of these, tourism is now a year round activity. This new trend of tourism has influenced the development and functional morphology of the town.

The impacts of these pressures are felt in varied ways and from varied directions. Services provided get multiplied if the watershed is also considered along with the water body. The water supply as well as the waste disposal system of Nainital town depends heavily upon the lake and its watershed. During the past few decades, increasing local population and the tourist influx into the Nainital watershed have severely impacted upon the water quality of the lake as well as the water resources in the watershed. A sizable fraction of domestic sewage was entering the lake through open sewers until recently. A large population of animals particularly dogs (pets and strays) and monkeys are also contributing to the organic burden as well as contamination into the lake.

Unauthorized construction in the catchment and around the lake has contributed in the past and is contributing substantially to the input of debris. As a result of these excesses, the lake is facing serious problem of eutrophication, heavy metal pollution and siltation. The steep hills surrounding the lake have immature topography and are prone to landslips and landslides. The multitudes of human activities in the watershed have increased the rate of erosion causing further problems of water supply and its quality. Efforts are being made (some since the British period) for the collection and treatment of domestic waste. But an integrated management plan, for the water resources of Lake and its watershed, has not yet been developed or even conceptualised.

LANDSIDES

The catchment is highly fragile and prone to land slips and landslides. Already 7 major landslides have occurred during the last century or so (in 1867, 1880, 1890, 1924, 1982, 1987 and 1998). A number of debris has resulted from the recurring mass-movements in the lake basin. The biggest landslide occurred on 18 September 1880. The fall converted the North-Western part of the lake into a level tract, which is now called as the 'flats'. Nearly half of the human settlements in Nainital are on landslide debris deposited over the years. In fact, Lake originated as a result of differential vertical - rather rotational - movement along the Nainital Fault, which led to the impoundment of water of the stream flowing in the Naini valley.

The major landslide of 1880 on Sher-ka-Danda ridge (causing death of 151 persons including 43 Europeans) led to various activities relating to the development of watershed management practices such as construction of drainage network.

INSTABILITY OF HILLSLOPES

The hillsides around Nainital Lake are very unstable owing to the tectonic movement. Movements along the faults have weakened the rocks considerably. The instability of the hill sides is evident from the growing bulges on the hill slopes, the tilting of trees, the subsidence or sinking to lower levels of roads and pathways, the developing of cracks in buildings and other structures, and the movement of pillars. The instability has further increased owing to construction of heavy buildings in an unplanned manner and by cutting trees. The British as early as 1942 had suggested not constructing houses on slopes steeper than 26.5 degrees.

HIGH UNSTABLE ZONE

According to Professor K.S. Valdiya, and eminent geologist, the highly unstable zone consists the south west facing slopes of Sher-ka-Danda and a part of the north-east facing slope of the Priory Spur of Ayarpatta ridge. The Ballia gorge (deep narrowed valley with steep sides) below Tallital bus station and through which outflow of the lake water passes during the rains, also comes under the highly unstable zone.

The second highly unstable zone is on the south western side of the lake on the part of the priory-Fine View Spur above the *purda dhara*.

The third area of great instability is the upper reaches of the Ballia Ravine and the fourth is the south western facing scarp or steep slope of the Raj Bhawan-land's End tract. Blocks after blocks slump down the dangerous scarp or steep slope into the Nihal valley year after year.

MODERATELY UNSTABLE ZONE

The moderately unstable zones according to Professor Valdiya are those areas where no major landslides have occurred so far but the creep or gradual movement on the slopes is visible from the tilting of trees and cracks in the buildings etc. The area to the south-east of Assembly Cottage near Snow View up to the Municipal Library on the Mall Road can be taken as a moderately unsafe zone.

COMPARATIVELY SAFE ZONE

Prof. Valdiya is of the view that no part of Nainital can be described as totally free from hazards of slope failure. However, where the slope is gentler and less than 20 degrees, such as the Flats, Bara Bazaar, Sukhatal, Sleepy Hollow and Ardwell Camp, the present Uttarakhand Academy of Administration and surrounding area are comparatively stable so far as the slope failure is concerned.

LANDSLIDES IN THE RECENT PAST

Nainital has a long history of landslides and practically more than half the area of the Nainital Basin is covered with debris generated by landslides and erosion. As a matter of fact, the entire north-western and the south-eastern parts of Nainital are located on a succession of landslide debris fans. Professor K.S. Valdiya is of the view that the much deformed Nainital is naturally in an unstable condition. The acceleration of erosion and increased instability of hill slopes is owing to human activities, indiscriminate construction of heavy buildings in a much unplanned way and owing to the criminal disposal of debris, mostly on the drains and on the hill slopes.

In 1987 a massive landslide occurred in the Cheena peak Ridge, which threatened the existence of the buildings below the ridge. A portion on the top of the hill had caved in and a crack of about 65 meters in length, 1.5 meters in breadth and 2.5 meters deep had developed on the south west of Naina or Cheena ridge. The instability of the hill has been confirmed by several geologists.

The first warnings came on September 1987, when following heavy rains, boulders slipped from the Naina ridge, uprooting 100 trees. A few months later, on March 11, 1988 another major landslips occurred after a heavy rainfall and the rubble reached the town. But it were the landslides of July 4,5, and 6 1988, which did the maximum damage. On July 6th boulders, share and ruble slid down to the Melrose Compound and the Brook Hill Areas At 6.30 am, when the catastrophe ended, 61 buildings had been damaged affecting 470 families. It was estimated that 50,000 cubic meters of rock and shale had been displaced with over 15,000 cubic meters of rubble loosely resting on the catch walls, (built to trap falling debris) in the hill's upper reaches, creating an alarming situation.

The main cause of the land slide, which was pointed out by geologists was the blasting and felling of trees done to construct the 24 km stretch of road between Sukhatal and Vinayak. Its construction was started in 1976 and was completed in 1984.

Another reason of the landslide was the mushroom growth of houses in the Melrose Compound. In this area there were only two houses in 1950 but by 1987, the year when the landslide took place more than 200 houses had been constructed. Moreover some of the residents of the area while constructing their houses removed stones from the mullahs which drain the rain water. A few of the other residents and some contractors while working in the area took stones from the catch walls also, which had built to trap the falling debris. These stones as alleged by other residents of the area were used for construction by them.

On 21st June 1989, during the summer rains, shale and rubble from the Sher-ka-Danda ridge rolled down the hill and damaged two science laboratories and 10 rooms of CRST Intermediate College. Heavy construction and lack of proper drainage on Sher-ka-Danda was the main cause for the landslide. Further to promote tourism in Nainital, a ropeway was commissioned on Sher-ka-Danda Ridge in 1986. The very spot where the towers of the ropeway have been constructed is very close to the site of 1880 landslide in which 151 people died. Further the tower number two has already started showing signs of wear and tear. The hills in Nainital are very fragile and that is why the British dropped the Mountain Railway Scheme during the period, 1887-89. This year also some houses were damaged during the rainy season owing to the displacement of rubble.

On 24th July 1998 after excessive rains, a huge chunk of land slid down on the Government House road near the DSB Campus of Kumaun University. A creep had been observed near the DSB Campus two decades before the landslide took place. It was also reported that the creep had increased owing to heavy vehicular traffic and heavy construction. The weak physical structure had played an important role in causing the landslide. The adverse impact of unscientific and unplanned construction activities had substantially increased soil erosion and transported the harmful debris to the lake. Then there were no proper sewer lines and drains in the area. It seems that the sub-surface water due to seepage from soak pits and household drains increased the pore pressure and whatever drains were there got choked. Thus the continuous rains in July caused heavy runoff along the hill and triggered the landslide. Fortunately there was no loss of life.

After this incident, on 25th and 26th July, the same year, huge blocks of rocks toppled down the Camel's Back peak downwards into the Narain Nagar village to the south west of Nainital.

The Balianala mountainside witnessed landslides again in September, 2018. Worried over the dangers from the landslides here, a PIL was filed in the HC in September last year, urging the court to issue directions to the authorities concerned to take urgent steps for landslide mitigation in Nainital to avoid any major tragedy. On September 26, 2018, High Court of Uttarakhand constituted a high-power committee of experts for studying and suggesting a treatment plan for landslide-prone Balianala. The committee submitted its report to High Court on November 30, 2018. Under the directions of HC, many experts including those from Geological Survey of India (GSI) have surveyed the fragile slopes here since August last year.

UNCONTROLLED CONSTRUCTION

By the 1970s the construction of buildings had become uncontrolled and haphazard. In 1982 a total ban on construction of new commercial buildings was clamped. However, this was bypassed by taking a sanction for a residential building and then later converting into a commercial one. It was felt that the Municipality was incapable of monitoring and restricting the construction work and a more effective body for looking after Nainital and adjoining areas was proposed. As a result Greater Nainital Development Authority (GNDA) came into being in 1984 which had a few people's representatives. However, the scope of GNDA also encompassed the nearby villages and invited resistance from the village communities which led to the abandoning of GNDA in 1989. A new body called the Nainital Lake Regional Special Area Development Authority came into being later that year with the District Magistrate as its president.

The District Magistrate heading the Hill Side Safety Committee has all these departments under one roof but without having proper coordination among all. This leaves the Lake Nainital in a particularly vulnerable situation where no department is directly connected with its maintenance though all are somehow linked to it. The sudden spurt in tourism has led to a mad rush for constructing new hotels, guest houses and resorts in Nainital. In some cases, rules were being flouted in a brazen manner for illegal construction. According to data available from the Municipal Board in the 1950 there were 15 hotels in Nainital only, their number had rose up to 102 in 1981-82 and 134 in 1987-88.

At present the number of licensed/unlicensed hotels and guest houses, huge resorts calming star facilities in the Lake Basin and in lake region has reached around 200.The real-estate developers cashing in on the great demand for new houses have scarred the tender and lovely hill side and have constructed houses and huge hotels in localities which were declared unsafe and where such activities are strictly prohibited by the British and municipal bye-laws. Rubble from this work was not removed but dumped into the lake during the rains, which accelerate the rate of sedimentation.

To ensure the safety and stability of the hill slopes is to maintain a proper drainage system and to ensure the safety of the hill slopes. The good drainage system with 71 drains and 235 branches developed by the British by house and road builders with no arrangement of regular cleaning and periodical repair by the concerned departments that are supposed to maintain them. As a result the rain water infiltrates into the ground underneath through joints, fractures and cavities in the rocks causing landslides. Moreover the rain water finds its way through newly cut ground channels and thereby causing gully erosion through dense construction areas. The bridle paths do not have proper catch water side drains, so the paths become channels during heavy downpours. Further the infiltration of water from bathrooms and sanitary soak pits in areas without sewer lines, considerably increase the instability in some areas.

MAINTAINANCE OF DRAINAGE SYSTEM

The first and foremost thing to ensure the safety and stability of the hill slopes is to maintain a proper drainage system.

The good drainage system with 71 drains and 235 branches developed by the British by house and road builders with no arrangement of regular cleaning and periodical repair by the concerned departments that are supposed to maintain them. As a result the rain water infiltrates into the ground underneath through joints, fractures and cavities in the rocks causing landslides. Moreover the rain water finds its way through newly cut ground channels and thereby causing gully erosion through dense construction areas. The bridle paths do not have proper catch water side drains, so the paths become channels during heavy downpours. Further the infiltration of water from bathrooms and sanitary soak pits in areas without sewer lines, considerably increase the instability in some areas.

The focus has always been on checking construction activities or on upkeep of the drains but never has there been a concerted effort to consider the lake and its watershed as a whole keeping in view the ecological sensitivities of the entire situation. Few days back no particular department is responsible for this. The Irrigation Department is concerned only with the water in the lake and maintaining the sluice; the PWD is concerned with the maintenance of only the drains and the roads in the watershed; the Municipal Board is concerned only with cleaning activities and disposal of garbage and issuing of licenses of boats therein; while Jal Sansthan is concerned with supply of drinking water and maintenance of sewer lines, but is not concerned with maintaining the quality of water of the lake which it pumps. Now it is finally handed over to Irrigation Department with a hope of its conservation and revival.

Most of the population of the Lake Basin is dependent on these lakes for drinking water. During the last decades organic pollution in Nainital Lake has been increasing at a rate that even preliminary limnlogical studies show unmistakable symptoms. Certain toxic substances such as ammonia, hydrogen sulphide and methane, evolve round the year in the bottom layers and have affected fish population to a great extent. Fish mortality that was a casual phenomenon, especially in winter. The situation in other lakes is no better. It is high time that group-housing in the catchment areas of other lakes should be regulated and construction should be in consonance with the rules framed by the special Lake Area Development Authority, Nainital.

With the increase in population pressure and the resultant increased demand of shelter, arable land, grazing areas, fodder, fuel wood etc. along with special needs for tourism, the natural resources in this lake region of the Himalaya are being used erratically and ruthlessly, resulting, into environmental disruption and depleting of resource base. It is therefore increasingly realized that the formulation and implementation of the process of development planning, in the region, must be consistent with the natural resources base and its ecological productive potentials, so that the goal of ecologically sustainable development with economically viable growth could be attained. Since, land is the primary and fundamental natural resource, and it is the basis of the genesis, management and sustainable development of all other natural resources, land management has acquired critical importance in these fragile region The region therefore deserve specific attention and priority conservation measures for protecting the lakes and its environ.

RECOMMENDATIONS

Urbanization represents a revolutionary change in the whole pattern of social life. Itself it is a product of basic economy and technological developments; it tends in turn, once it comes into being to affect every aspect of existence. Even though the recognition of these and other conditions, the government has yet to create an urbanization adaptation plan for Nainital, a detailed vulnerability and disaster risk assessment needs to be carried out for the township. These and other urban development initiatives do not incorporate the impacts of urban ecosystem, nor do they include a mechanism for adaptation.

In view of this situation, the following

recommendations are made, particularly for the policy planning agencies at local, regional, state and national levels:

A comprehensive urban development vulnerability assessment and mapping of the town should be carried out, taking into account all the critical parameters of exposure, sensitivity, and adaptive capacity of the urban planning.

- A detailed and large-scale risk zone mapping of the town should be carried out, analyzing the parameters of geology, structure, demography, economy, and livelihood, infrastructure and services.
- A comprehensive urban land use policy should be developed and implemented, taking into account conservation, development, disaster risk reduction needs, and the priorities of the town.
- A participatory framework for the conservation of water resources, particularly through reducing anthropogenic intervention in the recharge zone of the Nainital Lake and Sukhatal, should be developed.
- An integrated plan must be formulated, incorporating the above-mentioned points and involving a range of institutions and stakeholders (e.g., government line departments, private enterprises, civil society and non-governmental organizations, community based organizations, and academic and research institutions).

The review of Master Plan of Nainital, the hill town of Uttarakhand, and its lake region plan revealed their concern towards landslide hazards. Geological Surveyor India had studied and identified instability of slope of the town. Complex folding and faulting has induced brittle ductile shear zones making this hard rock terrain susceptible to high degree of infiltration attendant with poor runoff. The Master Plan has declared the very high-risk zone as prohibited areas with certain Regulations, like no new construction, no renovation, etc. Even then the whole plan needs systematic efforts to mitigate such disaster, to direct ULB to remain prepared for such event, effective implementation of rules, awareness programmes, financing insurance against disaster and accountability.

FUTURE STRATEGIES

- Development in each planning zone in the Lake Region Area shall be in cognizance to its topography and geographical setting.
- Development of tourism based infrastructure to be promoted in Bhimtal and Naukuchiatal Lake area.
- Development of tourism and environmental friendly commercial activities to be promoted in Sattal Lake region.
- Bhowali lies in the centre of the Nainital Lake Region Special Development Area and has the capacity to fulfil the demands of high level government offices.
- Required development to the extent of its carrying capacity and surrounding areas of Khurpatal, Charkhet, Narayn Nagar,Manora, Takula, Baldiyakhan, Patwadangar, etc. should be developed to accommodate additional population growth. Khurpatal area is proposed to have development in the sectors of residential, tourism, parking, entertainment, government offices and commercial establishments.
- Apart from keeping the drains in proper shape by efficient maintenance and regular cleaning of screens and catch pits following measures are essential to be taken. Requirement for repairs and reconstruction of

drains in critical sections. Need for additional cross walls and catch pits and Non-existence of screens at outfalls. Non availability of cleaning platforms at coarse screens. Removal of obstruction in the road side drains. Disconnection of side drains from sewers.

- Absence of road hierarchy and inadequate traffic carrying capacity. Most of the internal roads are single lane except few roads, rapid growth of vehicles and population (both permanent and floating) result in exceeding the carrying capacity on the road network. Lack of enforcement measures has further deteriorated the situation. Encroachment on streets by shop owner and vendors further reduced the width of carriage way. Basic problem of traffic movement along major arterial road network is the absence of alternative road network. Hindrance of pedestrian movement because absence of footpaths. Absence of adequate parking lots leading to haphazard on-street parking reducing road capacity thereby causing traffic congestion. The Lack of public transport system in the city has resulted in improper operation of Intermediate Public Transport Vehicles causing traffic congestion and pollution. Ineffective traffic control and management measures. Inadequate road infrastructure, side protection barriers and the safety issue.
- Heritage components in the city which needs conservation efforts are required. Culture and traditions of Nainital is not generally exposed to public consciousness. This exposure can be achieved through an identification of the elements and local activities, weaving narratives around them and then presenting it to the public through diverse means that can be interpretation centres, experiential museums,

walks, publications etc. New elements that draw from the town's history and efficient public service systems can be developed to impact public as well as policy makers.

- Architectural elements: Roofing Pattern, Townscape, Buildings and areas of historical interest, Buildings and features of architectural interest, Wooden facades of houses, Street paving's, Water hydrants and spouts, Bridle paths. Buildings such as Churches, Old temple, school buildings, government buildings constructed in 'Nainital Style' and Cemeteries sites are needed to be conserved.
- Revival of water springs, revival of public parks, up gradation of sanitation facilities, the development of pedestrian walkways, roads and parking areas are need of the hour.

Nainital presents a representative illustration of the phenomenal urban growth that is taking places in the states of Himalayan Mountains of India, Pakistan, Bhutan and Nepal, and also in mountain regions across the developing world. The situation presented and recommendations made could be translated to a large number of mountain and hill townships all across the mountain ranges.

Bibliography

1. A short History of the Church of Saint John's in the Wilderness, Nainital, Kanpur Christ Church Mission Press 1914
2. Ajay S. Rawat and Deepak Singhal, Corbett's Nainital Travails of a Crumbling City, Nainital Lake Region Special Area Development Authority (NLRSADA), Nainital, 1998.
3. Ajay S. Rawat and S. Raju, Nainital Beckons, Nainital Lake Region Special Area Development Authority (NLRSADA), Nainital, 2010.
4. Almora town". The Imperial Gazetteer of India, Vol. 5. Oxford at Clarendon Press. 1909.p.252,http://dsal.uchicago.edu/reference/gazetteer/pager.html?objectid=DS405.1.I34_V21 _239.gif Retrieved on 10/10/2015
5. Atkinson E.T. the Himalayan Gazetteer, District of the North Western Provinces 1886
6. Atkinson, E.T. (1882) The Himalayan Districts of the North-Western Provinces of India, Vol. II. Reprinted as the Himalayan Gazetteer, Cosmos, Delhi, 1973.
7. Boerefijn, Wim (2010). The foundation, planning and

building of new towns in the 13th and 14th centuries in Europe. An architectural-historical research into urban form and its creation. Ph.d. Thesis Universiteit van Amsterdam. ISBN 978-90-9025157-8.

8. Clay, J. M., Nainital: A Historical and Descriptive Account, The Superintend Government Press, United Province, Allahabad, 1928
9. District Gazetteer of the United Provinces of Agra and Awadh, Supplementary Notes and District Statistics to Volume XXXIV, Nainital District. Superintendent Government Press, United Provinces 1925
10. District Gazetteer of the United Provinces of Agra and Awadh, Supplementary Notes and District Statistics up to 1931-32 to Volume XXXIV (D) Nainital District. Superintendent Government Press, United Provinces 1936
11. Executive Summary, Conservation and Management Plan for Nainital Lake
12. Giriraj Shah, Nainital: The Land of Trumpet and Song; based on J.M. Clay's book on Nainital, Abhinav Publications, 1999.
13. Gopal, Madan: K.S. Gautam, ed. India through the ages. Publication Division, Ministry of Information and Broadcasting, Government of India, 1990
14. Gupta et al., Limnology of Lakes.in S.P.Singh&Brij Gopal edited, Nainital and Kumaun Himalayan Lakes, WWF publication, 1999.
15. Gupta, P.K., S.S. Nagdali and S.P. Singh, Limnology of Lakes. In: Nainital and Kumaun Himalaya Lakes. Eds. S.P. Singh and Brij Gopal, NIE Publication, New Delhi, 1999.
16. Gupta, R.K. (1977) Watershed - The Right Approach to Ecosystem Management in the Himalayas. In: Dialogue, Paper Presented in a Seminar on Himalayan

Mountain Ecosystems, Max Mueller Bhawan, New Delhi, 142-154.

17. Index to Nainital State Plans Survey in Session 1867 and Bungalows in Nainital : Revenue Survey Sketch Guide Map for Cantonment and Settlement of Nainital States 1872 and other related reports
18. J.M. Clay, 'Nainital : A Historical and Descriptive Account' Government Press, United Provinces, Allahabad 1928 (Reprinted 'Pahar' Nainital 2010)
19. Joshi, S.C., Joshi, D.R. and Dani, D.D. (1983) Kumaun Himalaya: A geographical Perspective on Resource Development, GyanodayaPrakashan, Nainital.
20. K.S. Valdiya Geology and Natural Environment of Nainital Hills, Kumaun Himalaya Gyanodaya Prakashan, Nainital, 1998.
21. K.S. Valdiya Geology and Natural Environment of Nainital Hills, Kumaun Himalaya Gyanodaya Prakashan, Nainital 1998
22. Kolb, Frank (1984). Die Stadtim Altertum. München: Verlag C.H. Beck. pp. 51-141: Morris, A.E.J. (1972). History of Urban Form. Prehistory to the Renaissance. London. pp. 22-23.
23. L.D.A.Loktak, (1999), Loktak Lake in Paril, Newsletter, Wetland InternationalOct.1999, vol. 1, pp3.
24. M. S. Reddy and N.V.V.Char, Management of Lakes in India, 2004, Ministry of Water Resources, Government of India, New Deldi
25. Metal fractionation study on bed sediments of Lake Nainital, National Institute of Hydrology, Roorkee, Uttaranchal, India
26. Nagarpalika, Nainital's yearly reports
27. Nainital : The District Gazetteer of the United Provinces of Agra and Awadh, Supplementary Notes and Statistics to Volume XXXIV, of Government Press

United Provinces, Allahabad, 1917

28. Nainital Municipal Board By Laws 1966
29. Nevill, H.R. , Nainital Gazetteer- XXXIV, first published in 1904, reprinted by Natraj Publishers, Dehradun, 2016
30. NIH Report (1999) Hydrological studies of Lake Nainital, Kumaun Himalayas Uttar Pradesh (1998-1999), National Institute of Hydrology, Roorkee (U.P.).
31. Pandey Prayag, Nainital Ek Dharohar, Consul Press, Nainital, 2016
32. Pandey, B.D, History of Kumaun English version of Kumaun ka Itihas Badri Dutt Pande, Translated by C.M. Agarwal, Shyam Prakashan, Shree Almora Book Depot, Almora, 1993
33. Pilgrim- Notes of Wanderings in the Himalayas (Agra News Press, Agra- 1844)
34. Public Work Department, Kumaun Division 'Regulation in Connection with Hill Side Safety and Lake Control', Nainital, United Provinces, Allahabad 1932
35. Ranikhet: The Imperial Gazetteer of India, v. 21, p. 233, http://dsal.uchicago.edu/reference/gazetteer/pager.html?objectid=DS405.1.I34_V21_239.g if retrived on 10/10/2017
36. Rawat A.S. & Deepak Singhal (1998), Corbetts Nainital, Travails of a Crumbling City, NLRSDA, Nainital, p p73-83.
37. Rawat, Ajay Singh: Almoriana : A Travel Account of Kumaun Himalayan Ranges (leaves from a Hill Journal), Gyanodaya Prakashan, 1991.
38. Rawat, Ajay, Magnificent Nainital, Uttarakhand Police, Nainital
39. Rawat, J.S. (1987) Morphology & Morphometry of the Lake Naini, Kumaun, Lesser Himalaya. Journal of the Geological Society of India, 30:493-498.

40. Recommendation of Brijendra Sahay of Committee 1994-95
41. Regional Archives, Nainital
42. Report, Water Quality of Nainital Lakes as reflected by physico-chemical parameters of the lake water during 2003-04 to 2010-11, Kumaun University, Nainital
43. Sah Reetesh, *An Account of Himalayan State of Uttarakhand with special reference to Regional History'* published in the Proceedings of UGC sponsored National Seminar on The Importance of Regional History in Modern Age,4 April, 2015, at Warora, Chandrapur (Maharashtra) ISBN No.- 978-93-82405-22-1
44. Sah Reetesh,'*History of Uttarakhand'* published in the Abstract Volume of Seminar on "Magamatism, Tectonism and Mineralization (MTM 2007). Organized by Department of Geology, Kumaun University and X Annual Convention of South Asian Association of Economic Geologists, 29-31 October 2007
45. Sah Reetesh, Education System in Nainital During the Nineteenth and Mid-Twentieth Century British India, QUEST, The Journal of UGC-HRDC, Nainital, Vol.-11, Issue-3, September-December 2017
46. Shah G.L. and Ajay S. Rawat, Uttranchal : A New Himalayan Entity, Souvenir, North Zone Vice-Chancellor Conference, Kumaun University, Nainital 2006
47. Shah Griraj, Abode of Gods: Uttarakhand, Cosmo Publications, New Delhi, 1984
48. Shah, G.L., Nainital : SamaykaEk Kaleidoscope, AmolikaPrakashan, Nainital, 2016
49. Shanker D. Bhatt, Ravindra K. Pande, Ecology of the Mountain Waters, Ashish Publishing House, New

Delhi, 1991

50. Sharad Nanda (Sharadotsav Souvenir, 1998, 2000, 2004, 2005 and 2013)
51. Singh Kulwant&Florina Steinberg edtd.,1998;Urban India in Crisis, HSMI Delhi &HIS Rotterdom, NAILPub. New Delhi
52. Singh S.P.& Brijgopal,2002 IMLLNW, Final Report of the World Bank aided Technical Assistance Project," Indian Environmental Capacity Building".
53. Singh, S.P. (2002) Balancing the approaches of environmental conservation by considering ecosystem services as well as biodiversity. Current Science, 82 (11): 1331-1335.
54. Singh, S.P. and Brij Gopal, Nainital and Himalayan Lakes (eds.), NIE and WWF, New Delhi, 1999.
55. Souvenir Nainital Yatch Club, Nainital 1990
56. Surendra Nath, Recent Advances in Fish Ecology, Limnology and Eco-Conservation, Volume 3, Daya Publishing House , New Delhi, 1994
57. Taylor, Nigel (2007). Urban Planning Theory since 1945, London, Sage.
58. Uttar Pradesh District Gazetteer, Nainital, Editor: Vanarasi Das, Government Press, Allahabad, Uttar Pradesh 1992
59. Van Assche, K., Beunen, R., Duineveld, M., & de Jong, H. (2013). Co-evolutions of planning and design: Risks and benefits of design perspectives in planning systems. Planning Theory, 12(2), 177-198.
60. W, Walker, MD, Angling in the Kumaun Lakes, 1888, Republished by PaharPothi, 2010.
61. Waldiya K.S. : 'PathriliPagdandiyon Par' Published : Pahar- 2015
62. Waldiya K.S.1988, Geology and Natural Environment of Nainital Hills, Kumaun Himalaya; Gyanodaya

Prakashan, Nainital.

WEBSITES

- http://nainital.nic.in
- http://www.worldlakes.org
- http://moef.nic.in
- http://wikipedia.org
- http://www.kbinirsnb.be
- www.planning.org
- www.pahar.in

Photographs

- Re-photographed from the collection of Sh. P.L. Sah
- Courtesy: Internet
- Personal Collection

ANNEXURE-I

Estate Plan of Nainital, 1867

S. No.	Name of Estate	Details of allocated Land		
		Acre	Road	Pole
1	Cheena Park	21	3	38
2	Ardwell	15	1	08
3	Peters' Field	3	2	24
4	Ash dale	6	1	30
5	Brooke hill	17	1	19
6	Ash dale Cottage			
7	Dunedin House	6	2	32
8	Fair light	11	3	14
9	Assembly Cottage			
10	Fair Hall	10	3	28
11	Sher -KaDanda			
12	Bride House	0	3	26
13	Windermere	4	2	32
14	Annandale	9	0	00
15	Grasmere			

16	Hermitage	32	3	00
17	The Wish rage	4	0	17
18	Sleepy Hallow			
19	The Retreat	4	0	17
20	Belvedere	7	1	36
21	Vienna Lodge	9	2	21
22	Long dale	5	3	32
23	Spring Cottage	3	3	19
24	The Prairie Estate	18	0	30
25	Strawberry Lodge State	9	1	05
26	Prairie Cottage			
27	Strawberry Hall			
28	New Hall			
29	Strawberry Lodge			
30	Spring Field			
31	Alma Cottage	3	1	3
32	Pilgrim Cottage	4	0	18
33	Alma Lodge			
34	Garden House			
35	Hawthorn Dane	2	1	03
36	Oak Lodge	13	2	21
37	Baler House	9	0	14
38	Cheena Lodge	2	1	16
39	Bray side			
40	Himalaya House			
41	Side Ayarpata			
42	Hawthorn Den Cottage	0	2	37
43	Role Strone Side	6	1	32
44	Oak Cottage			
45	Role Stone House			

46	Northern Lodge	5	3	33
47	Stoneleigh/Rohila Lodge	15	3	09
48	Coober field House	4	3	03
49	Wood land	3	1	28
50	Coober Field Cottage			
51	Vilathye Cottage	4	1	37
52	Emily Lodge	3	3	06
53	Side Over Jai Kishan Cottage			
54	Emily Cottage			
55	Cypress Cottage	0	1	32
56	Edwin Cottage	3	2	29
57	Sunny Side	0	3	34
58	Edwin Lodge			
59	Pilgrim Lodge	2	2	14
60	Glenmore	5	0	00
61	Seven Oaks	8	1	32
62	End leaf	13	0	06
63	End wine Stove	0	1	34
64	Cypress Lodge	3	2	29
65	Hope Cottage			
66	Bell view (West)	1	3	16
67	Doubly Grove			
68	South Wood State	1	3	16
69	I.V. Park -1	6	0	16
70	Ramnee	30	0	22
71	I.V. Park -2			
72	Bhabar Cottage	3	0	10
73	Long View Donaldabad	28	1	09
74	Lake Side/Mall House	2	1	37
75	Balham House	5	3	30

76	Rock House State	5	2	33
77	Bank House	2	1	19
78	Side Sher-KaDanda	9	3	14
79	No. 2 Ayarpata	7	0	11
80	Oak Park			
81	Marshal Cottage	5	1	22
82	Mission Warrior Ground	0	2	20
83	Nor flack House	4	2	22
84	Clop stoke Lodge	8	1	19
85	Charlton Lodge	5	3	20
86	Clop stock Cottage			
87	Side Sher KaDanda	1	3	32
88	Victoria Hotel			
89	Malden	19	0	18
90	Waverly Cottage (I.V. Park - 3)			
91	Side Sher-KaDanda	4	1	08
92	Saint Loo	14	2	32
93	Ravens wood (ShukhNivas)	8	2	38
94	Omnibus	3	2	36
95	Danda House	14	1	11
96	Telegraph House	6	1	10
97	Omnibus Cottage			
98	Lake House (Harish Hotel)			
99	Over shier House			
100	Side Ayarpata	3	2	16
101	Melville Hall	2	2	00
102	Number 1 Rookery	1	3	20
103	Wilding Lodge	5	0	11
104	Number 2 Rookery			
105	Helen Villa			

106 Glean Ville (Methodist Church)	0	3	02
107 Side Sher kadanda	27	0	06
108 Smugglers Retreat	18	1	24
109 Smugglers Hall	3	0	25
110 Ewan Ho	2	0	33
111 Sherwood/Land Slip House	25	2	22
112 Rolleston	1	0	04
113 Alma House	2	1	37
114 Jai Kishan Cottage	3	0	25
115 Oak Cottage			
116 Bow Cottage	8	0	02
117 The Ruin	7	1	16
118 Edge Hill			
119 Side Sher KaDanda	7	2	08
120 Prim Rose Cottage	2	0	20
121 Cypress Lodge	2	3	20
122 Albany Cottage	2	0	00
123 Buttress Castle	2	1	12
124 Lake View			
125 Cal stone	16	1	35
126 Kill stone Side	6	0	27
127 Pear Tree House			
128 Prospect lodge	4	0	03
129 St. Helens'	2	2	36
130 Rook Wood	2	1	28
131 Side Sher Ka Daanda (Mr. Frazer)	9	1	33
132 Side Sher ka Daanda			
133 The Pavilion			
134 Ayarpata	26	0	07
135 Daak Bangla	1	1	05

136 St. Johns Church	7	3	08
137 Pops Villa	2	2	19
138 The Abbey	4	0	30
139 Ovary Villa			
140 St. Leonard			
141 Ojale Grove (Commissioner office)	5	2	1
142 Rajpur	2	1	24
143 Side Cheena Slope	4	1	07
144 Glencoe			
145 Over Seer house	1	0	3
146 Nainital Bazar	27	0	11
147 Tallital Bazar			
148 Rohilla Lodge			
149 Hill View			
150 Stone Gross			
151 Vernon Cottage			
152 Eastern House			
153 The Chase			
154 New Berry Lodge			
155 Livy Cottage			
156 Star And Grater Hotel			
157 Melville Lodge/Fire Tree House	7	2	10
158 Lake View	4	0	08
159 Forest lodge	4	1	03
160 Springdale	8	2	18
161 Fairy Lodge	4	1	6
162 Tarai Office			
163 Fairy Hall			
164 Side Sher ka Danda	5	2	18
165 Dalhousie	11	0	00

166 Darrin Castle			
167 Stone Cross			
168 Club (Nainital Club)			
169 Bridge House	0	3	26

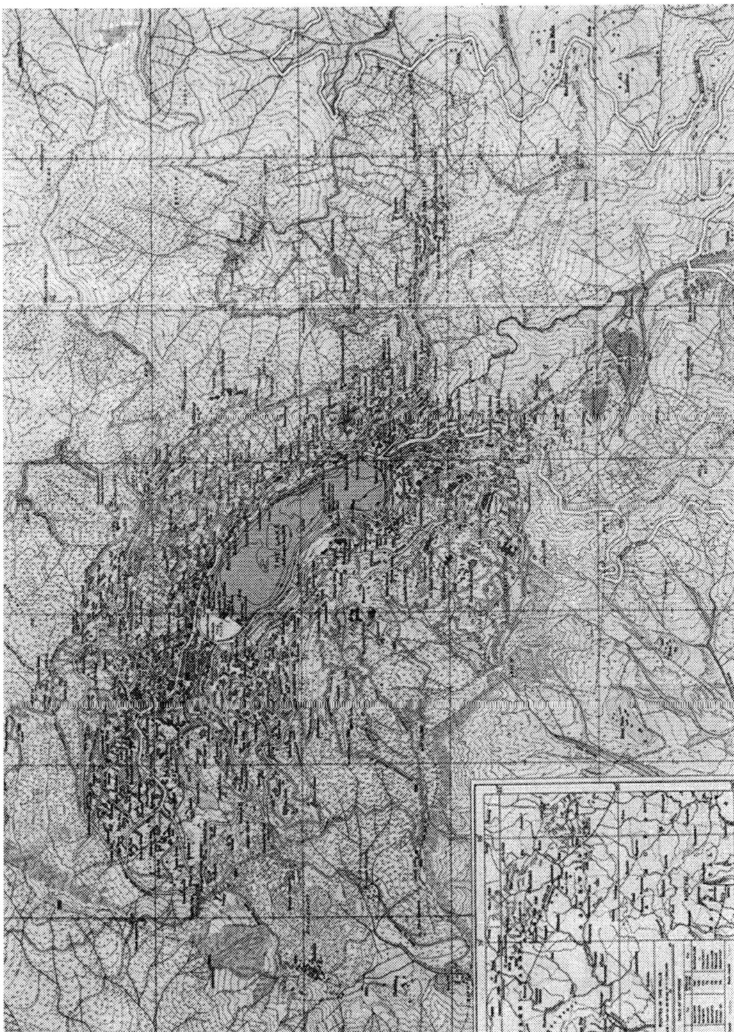

ANNEXURE-II

Geological Map and Sections of Nainital Geological Survey of India XXXIII

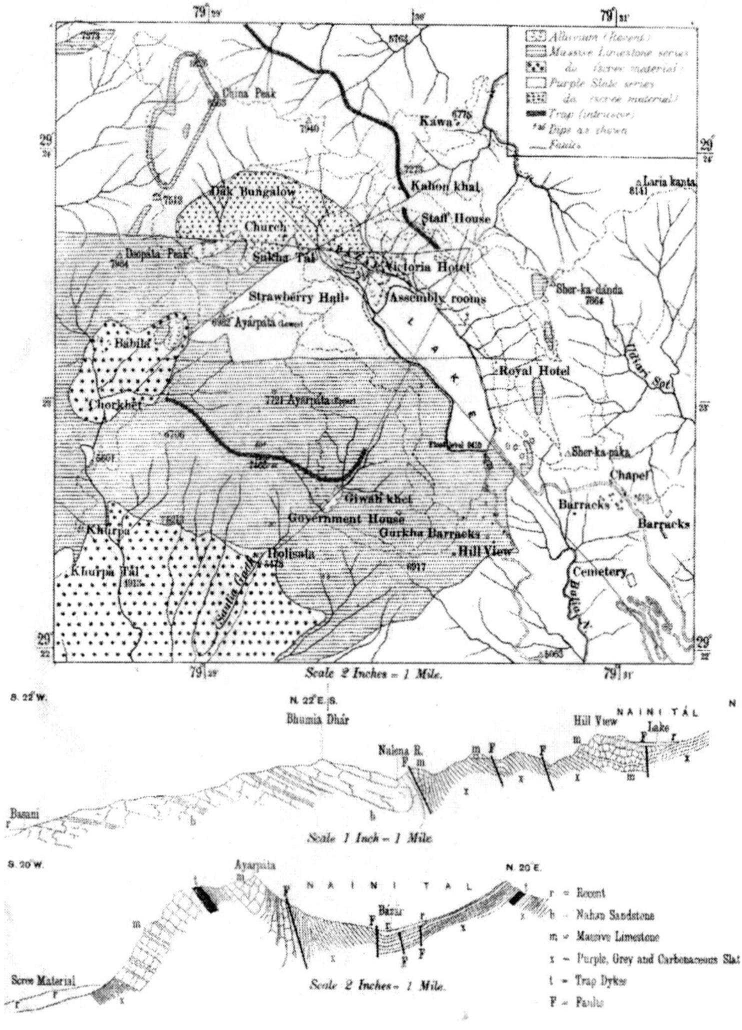